Rhymes for Circle Time

A fantastic collection of finger plays & action rhymes

By
Louise Binder Scott

Cover illustration by
Jalie Anderson

Inside illustrations by
Teena Hahn

Publisher
Instructional Fair • TS Denison
Grand Rapids, Michigan 49544

Instructional Fair • TS Denison

All finger plays and rhymes in this book are the author's
original contributions unless specified otherwise.

Dedication

In loving memory of Louise Binder Scott
whose delightful action rhymes and finger plays
truly entertain young children

Instructional Fair • TS Denison Staff

Credits

Author: Louise Binder Scott
Cover Artist: Julie Anderson
Inside Illustrations: Teena Hahn
Project Director/Editor: Debra Olson Pressnall
Cover Art Direction: Darcy Bell-Myers
Graphic Layout: Deborah Hanson McNiff

About the Author

Louise Binder Scott (Ed.M., Boston University; former speech-language-hearing-reading specialist, San Marino Schools, California; former Associate Professor of Speech Education, California State University) was the author of many publications for early childhood educators.

Standard Book Number: 1-56822-811-2
Rhymes for Circle Time
Copyright © 1999 by Ideal • Instructional Fair Publishing Group
a division of Tribune Education
2400 Turner Avenue NW
Grand Rapids, Michigan 49544

Table of Contents

Childhood is a time of wonderment, curiosity, and investigation. To childhood also belongs the realm of "let's pretend." In this world of make-believe, animals talk, boxes become airplanes, and sticks turn into horses. Here, too, the magic of imagination converts small fingers into rabbits and kittens. By making a circle with her arms, the child has created the sun, or a ball, or even a snow-person. Everything children do provides situations from which they learn. Through play, they gain a favorable self-concept, for they can express freely and conduct their experiments in constructive ways, control their primitive emotions, and gain satisfaction in their own abilities. Eventually, they can attain a basis for abstract thinking and spatial relationships, and can converse and share with others.

Finger plays and action rhymes have descended through the ages and are found in most countries of the world. Their perpetuation appears to be due to the physical and close contact of the parent-child relationships in which the family is involved. To the parent, finger plays are a way of helping the child move toward self-discovery and mastery over the movements of his fingers, hands, and arms. To the teacher, finger plays have many additional values. The manual dexterity and muscular control acquired in the earlier finger games played with the parent can be utilized and expanded into an understanding of rhythm—the rhythm of speech and music, the rhythm of life's activities.

Teaching finger plays and action rhymes requires a number of simple techniques. Although each "game" has certain individual elements, the following list of suggestions will help the teacher in presenting the rhymes.

1. If you are facing the child or a group of children, you should mirror the actions which you wish the child to perform. For example, if you wish the child to use her right hand, you should hold up your left hand. Children will tend to move in the same direction as the demonstrator facing them. The teacher, then, must make his movements in the reverse of those expected from the group.

2. Be aware, too, of the fact that there may be children in the group who are left-handed. These children may perform certain right-handed movements in an awkward manner. If you sense a coordination problem, suggest to the child that he, too, face the class.

3. Have the children follow only the action until they understand what they are to do during the rhyme or finger play. After they have played the "game" once, they will be able to say a few of the words after you.

4. Provide for several repetitions of each finger play before going on to another. Children will need to repeat the rhyme in order to learn it. As the rhyme becomes more familiar, children will ask to do it over and over again.

5. Have fun with these rhymes and the child will respond to your enthusiasm.

Animals

Swinging Birds

Two tall telephone poles,
(Hold up hands, palms inward,
pointer finger erect.)
Across them a wire is strung;
(Extend middle fingers until they touch at tips.)
Two little birds hopped on,
(Move thumbs to touch extended middle fingers.)
And swung and swung and swung.
(Swing hands back and forth.)
—*Traditional*

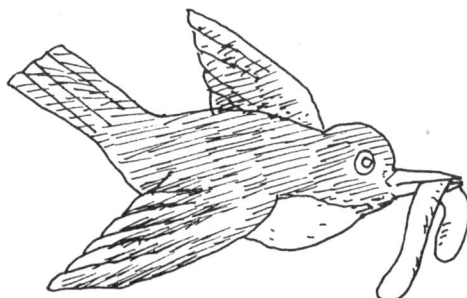

Seven Plump Robins

Seven plump robins were hopping all around,
Picking up bread crumbs off the ground.
Two saw a yellow cat up in a tree.
Two flew away, then there were three!
One heard a black cat say, "Mew, Mew,"
He flew away, then there were two.
One saw a striped cat sitting in the sun.
One saw a white cat and she began to run.
Now there were no robins hopping all around,
Picking up bread crumbs off the ground.
(Show the designated number of fingers each time.
Children may supply the number remaining.)

Five Little Robins

Five little robins in a sycamore tree,
A father,
(Hold up thumb.)
A mother,
(Hold up pointer finger.)
And babies three;
(Hold up remaining fingers.)
Father brought a worm,
(Point to thumb.)
Mother brought a bug;
(Point to pointer finger.)
The three baby robins started to tug;
This one ate the bug,
(Point to middle finger.)
This one ate the worm,
(Point to ring finger.)
And this one sat and waited for his turn.
(Point to little finger.)

Fly, Little Bird

Fly, little bird. Go back to your tree.
(Motion of flying.)
That's where your baby birds ought to be.
The tree branches sway from side to side.
(Sway body back and forth.)
But your dear baby birds are safe inside.
(Close fists.)
Their nest is as snug as snug can be
(Cup hands.)
Away up in a tall apple tree.
(Point upward.)

Here Is a Bunny

Here is a bunny with ears so funny;
(Two fingers up straight.)
Here is his hole in the ground;
(Make circle of forefinger and thumb.)
Up go his ears and he runs to his hole,
(Motion of running fingers.)
When he hears a strange little sound.
(Clap hands.)
—*Traditional*

Bunny, Bunny

Bunny, white bunny
(Place pointer fingers beside head.)
With ears so tall.
And your two pink eyes
And a mouth so small.
(Make "O" with mouth.)
Wiggle goes one ear.
(Wiggle one finger.)
Wiggle goes the other.
(Wiggle other finger.)
Hop, hop, hop, hop
Home to your mother!
(Hop away in four hops.)

This Little Bunny

This little bunny has two pink eyes;
(Hold up fingers of one hand; point to forefinger.)
This little bunny is very wise;
(Point to middle finger.)
This little bunny is soft as silk;
(Point to ring finger.)
This little bunny is white as milk;
(Point to little finger.)
This little bunny nibbles away
(Point to thumb.)
At cabbages and carrots the live-long day!

Five Little Bunnies

Five little bunnies are such dears!
The first little bunny has pink ears.
(Hold up a finger at each side of head.)
The second little bunny has soft toes.
(Point to feet.)
The third little bunny sniffs with her nose.
(Make two sniffs.)
The fourth little bunny is very smart.
(Point to forehead.)
The fifth little bunny has a loving heart.
(Place hand over heart.)

(This rhyme can be used as a finger play or acted out.)

Once There Was a Bunny

Once there was a bunny,
(Double left fist and extend two fingers for ears.)
And a green, green cabbage head;
(Double fist on right hand.)
"I think I'll have some breakfast," the little bunny said;
(Move bunny toward cabbage head.)
So he nibbled and he nibbled,
(Move fingers on left hand.)
Then he turned around to say,
"I think this is the time I should be hopping on my way!"
(Make hopping movements with left hand.)
—*Traditional*

Five Little Rabbits

Five little rabbits under a log;
(Hold up fingers of one hand.)
This one said, "Sh! I hear a dog!"
(Point to forefinger.)
This one said, "I see a man!"
(Point to middle finger.)
This one said, "I'm not afraid!"
(Point to thumb.)
A man and his dog went hurrying by,
And you should have seen those rabbits fly!

Twelve Little Rabbits

Twelve little rabbits in a rabbit pen;
Two hopped away and then there were ten.
(Hold up ten fingers.)
Ten little rabbits with ears up straight;
Two hopped away and then there were eight.
(Bend down two fingers.)
Eight little rabbits doing funny tricks;
Two hopped away and then there were six.
(Bend down two fingers.)
Six little rabbits eating carrots from the store;
Two hopped away and then there were four.
(Bend down two fingers.)
Four little rabbits looked for gardens new;
Two hopped away and then there were two.
(Bend down two fingers.)
Two little rabbits found a new friend;
They hopped away, and that is the end.
(Bend down last two fingers.)

The Rabbits

A family of rabbits lived under a tree;
(Close right hand and hide it under left arm.)
A father, a mother, and babies three.
(Hold up thumb, then fingers in succession.)
Sometimes the bunnies would sleep all day;
(Make fist.)
But when night came, they liked to play.
(Wiggle fingers.)
Out of the hold they'd go creep, creep, creep,
(Move fingers in creeping motion.)
While the birds in the trees were all asleep.
(Place palms together, rest face on hands.)
Then the bunnies would scamper about and run . . .
(Wiggle fingers.)
Uphill, downhill! Oh, what fun!
(Move fingers vigorously.)
But when the mother said, "It's time to rest,"
(Hold up middle finger.)
Pop! They would hurry
(Clap hands after "Pop!")
Right back to their nest!
(Hide hand under arm.)

Ten Huge Dinosaurs

Ten huge dinosaurs were standing in a line.
One tripped on a cobblestone and then there were _____.

Nine huge dinosaurs were trying hard to skate.
One cracked right through the ice, and then there were _____.

Eight huge dinosaurs were counting past eleven.
One counted up too far, and then there were _____.

Seven huge dinosaurs learned some magic tricks,
One did a disappearing act, and then there were _____.

Six huge dinosaurs were learning how to drive.
One forgot to put in gas, and so then there were _____.

Five huge dinosaurs joined the drum corps.
One forgot the drumsticks, and then there were _____.

Four huge dinosaurs were wading in the sea.
One waded too far out, and then there were _____.

Three huge dinosaurs looked for Mister Soo.
One gave up the search, and then there were _____.

Two huge dinosaurs went to the Amazon.
One sailed in up to his head, and then there was _____.

One lonesome dinosaur knew his friends had gone.
He found a big museum, and then there were _____.
—*Adapted from an old English rhyme*

(Children may supply the number remaining.)

Five Little Owls

This little owl has great, round eyes.
This little owl is of very small size.
This little owl can turn her head.
This little owl likes mice, she said.
This little owl flies all around,
And her wings make hardly a single sound.
   (Point to one finger at a time.)

Busy Squirrel

The little gray squirrel makes a scampering sound
   (Wiggle fingers.)
As she gathers the nuts that fall to the ground.
   *(Hold fingers high and let them move as
   they descend.)*
She buries the nuts in a secret dark place
   (One hand over other.)
And covers them with hardly a trace.
Little gray squirrels always seem to know
That the robins have gone and it's time for snow.
   (Raise arms and let fingers move as they descend.)

Squirrel in a Tree

This is the squirrel that lives in a tree;
   (Make fist; hold two fingers erect.)
This is the tree which he climbs;
   (Motion of fingers climbing up opposite arm.)
This is the nut that he takes from me;
   (Make small circle.)
As I sit very still sometimes.
   (Fold hands.)

Five Little Squirrels

Five little squirrels lived up in a tree.
   (Hold up five fingers.)
And they were alike as squirrels could be.
The first little squirrel was alone one day.
   (Point to one finger at a time.)
He called to his friends, "Come on and play!"
The second little squirrel jumped down from a limb.
The first little squirrel jumped after him.
The third little squirrel found nuts to eat.
He cracked them and oh, they tasted sweet.
The fourth little squirrel played hide and seek.
She hid her eyes and she did not peek.
The fifth little squirrel called, "Chirr-chirr-chirr-eee,"
And all of the squirrels came back to the tree.
   (Hold up five fingers.)

Baby Porcupine

Little baby porcupine,
What is on your back?
They are quills and every quill
Is sharper than a tack.
   (Hold up ten fingers for quills.)

Things That Hop

Here is a froggie, hippety-hop;
   (Make arms leap forward.)
With a hop,
   (One big hop.)
And a stop,
And a hop,
   (Another big hop.)
And a stop!

I Am a Little Toad

I am a little toad,
Hopping down the road.
   (Make fingers hop in time to verses.)
Just listen to my song;
I sleep all winter long;
   (Palms together at side of head.)
When spring comes, I peep out,
   (Peep behind hands.)
And then I jump about;
   (Make arms jump.)
And now I catch a fly,
   (Clap hands.)
And now I wink my eye;
   (Wink one eye.)
And now and then I hop,
   (Make hands hop.)
And now and then I stop!
   (Fold hands.)
     —Old rhyme

Dive, Little Tadpole

Dive, little tadpole, one;
   (Hold up one finger.)
Dive, little tadpoles, two;
   (Hold up two fingers.)
Swim, little tadpoles, Oh, oh, oh!
   (Clap three times.)
Or I will catch YOU!
   (Point.)

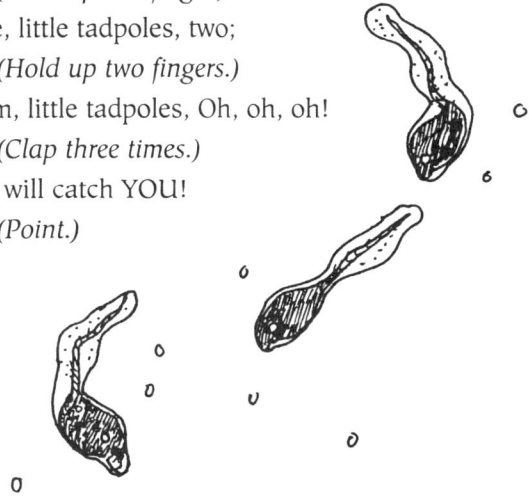

Ten Little Froggies

Ten little froggies were swimming in a pool.
   (Hold up ten fingers.)
This little froggie said, "Let's go to school!"
   (Point to thumb.)
This little froggie said, "Oh, yes! Let's go!"
   (Point to pointer finger.)
This little froggie said, "We'll sit in a row."
   (Point to middle finger.)
This little froggie said, "We'll learn to read."
   (Point to ring finger.)
This little froggie said, "Yes, yes, indeed."
   (Point to little finger.)
This little froggie said, "We'll learn to write."
   (Point to thumb on other hand.)
This little froggie said, "We'll try with all our might."
   (Point to pointer finger.)
This little froggie said, "We will draw and sing."
   (Point to middle finger.)
This little froggie said, "We'll learn EVERYTHING!"
   (Point to ring finger.)
This little froggie said, "Then after school,
   (Point to little finger.)
We'll come back here and swim in our pool."
   (Make swimming motions with fingers.)

Five Little Mice

Five little mice on the pantry floor;
(Hold up five fingers.)
This little mouse peeked behind the door;
(Bend down little finger.)
This little mouse nibbled at the cake;
(Bend down ring finger.)
This little mouse not a sound did make;
(Bend down middle finger.)
This little mouse took a bite of cheese;
(Bend down pointer finger.)
This little mouse heard the kitten sneeze.
(Bend down thumb.)
"Ah-choo!" sneezed Kitten, and "Squeak!" they cried,
As they found a hole and ran inside.
*(Make running motion with fingers and hide hand
behind back.)*

Where Are the Baby Mice?

Where are the baby mice?
Squeak, squeak, squeak!
(Make fist and hide it behind you.)
I cannot see them;
Peek, peek, peek!
(Show fist and extend it.)
Here they come out of their hole in the wall.
One, two, three, four, five, and that is all!
(Show one finger at a time.)

The Adventures of Little Mice

Five little mice looked for something to eat.
They wanted to have a wonderful treat.
The first little mouse nibbled at a slice
Of warm, fresh bread and it tasted nice.
The second little mouse nibbled at a cake.
He ate fast and got a tummy ache.
The third little mouse nibbled at a pie.
It tasted sweet and she gave a sigh.
The fourth little mouse nibbled at a cheese.
The fifth little mouse said, "Be quiet, please.
I hear someone coming to open the door!"
So they all hid under a board in the floor.
*(Five children dramatize the rhyme. It can be used
as a finger play; point to one finger at a time.)*

Tippy, Tippy Tiptoe

Tippy, tippy tiptoe,
There they go;
Ten little hungry mice
Walking in a row.
(Move fingers of both hands to right.)
They couldn't find a thing to eat,
And so they had to go
Tippy, tippy tiptoe,
(Move ten fingers to the left.)
Tippy, tippy tiptoe,
Tippy, tippy tiptoe . . .
—Adapted from an old English rhyme

What the Animals Do

We'll hop, hop, hop like a bunny,
    (Make hopping motion with hand.)
And run, run, run like a dog;
    (Make a running motion with fingers.)
We'll walk, walk, walk like an elephant,
    (Make walking motion with arms.)
And jump, jump, jump like a frog;
    (Make jumping motions with arms.)
We'll swim, swim, swim like a goldfish,
    (Make swimming motion with hand.)
And fly, fly, fly like a bird;
    (Make flying motion with arms.)
We'll sit right down and fold our hands,
    (Fold hands in lap.)
And not say a single word!

Two Little Turtles

One little turtle lived in a shell,
And that was a home
That he liked very well.
    (Make a fist for the shell.)
He poked out his head
    *(Thumb protrudes between middle finger
    and forefinger.)*
To look at the view.
Another turtle joined him
    *(Thumb protrudes between middle finger
    and forefinger on other hand.)*
And that made two.
They had small tails,
Their feet made tracks,
    (Wiggle fingers.)
And both of the turtles carried home on their backs.

Five Little Bears

Five little bears were sitting on the ground.
    (Five children sit in a row.)
Five little bears made a deep growling sound: Grrrrrr!
    (Children growl.)
The first one said, "Let's have a look around."
    (One child at a time rises.)
The second one said, "I feel rather funny!"
The third one said, "I think I smell honey."
The fourth one said "Shall we climb up the tree?"
The fifth one said, "Look out! There's a bee!"
So the five little bears went back to their play,
    (Children return to seats.)
And decided to wait till the bees flew away.

The Animals

I saw one hungry little mouse.
Squeak, squeak, squeak!
I said, "There's cheese inside my house."
Squeak, squeak, squeak!
I saw two funny little moles. Creep, creep, creep!
I said, "I'll help you dig your holes
Deep, deep, deep!"
I saw three frogs beside three logs.
Glug, glug, glug!
I fed some bugs to the hungry frogs.
Glug, glug, glug!
Four little fish swam with a swish.
Glip, glip, glup!
I fed some seaweed to the fish.
Glip, glip, glup!
I said, "Here rabbits, come and eat."
Nibble, nibble, nibble.
I fed five rabbits carrots sweet.
Nibble, nibble, nibble.
Six butterflies said, "Come and fly."
Flutter, flutter, fly!
I went to fly with the butterflies.
Flutter, flutter, fly!
    *(Children show designated number of fingers
    and say the animal's sound or refrain.)*

Elephants

One little elephant was playing in the sun.
(Child walks around ring.)
He thought that playing was such a lot of fun,
He called another elephant and asked him to come.
(A second child joins first.)
Two little elephants were playing in the sun.
They thought that playing was such a lot of fun,
They called another elephant and asked her to come.
(A third child joins in.)
Three little elephants were playing in the sun.
They thought that playing was such a lot of fun,
They called another elephant and asked him to come.
(A fourth appears.)
*(Continue the game, adding more children until
ten are participating. End the rhyme in this way:)*
Ten little elephants were playing in the sun.
They thought that playing was such a lot of fun,
They didn't call another elephant to come.
—*A traditional English rhyme*
*(Choose ten more children, so each will
have a turn.)*

The Elephant

The elephant has a trunk for a nose,
And up and down is the way it goes;
*(Clasp hands together, extend arms,
and raise and lower them.)*
He wears such a saggy, baggy hide!
(Relax body.)
Do you think two elephants would fit inside?
(Hold up two fingers.)

Rhinoceros

A rhinoceros, a rhinoceros
Sometimes he makes a dreadful fuss.
He has a big horn on his nose.
(Extend pointer finger from nose.)
He snorts and rumbles as he goes.
(Children say, "Grrrump!")
He's very long and very wide.
(Measure length and width with hands.)
He has a very wrinkled hide.
(Wavy motion with hands.)
He has big hoofs on his four feet.
(Hold up four fingers.)
We feed him grass and hay to eat.
A rhinoceros, a rhinoceros
Is surely not a pet for us.
(Shake head negatively.)

Kangaroo

Old hoppity-loppity kangaroo
Can jump much faster than I or you.
Hoppity-loppity, jump, one-two.
Her tail is bent like a kitchen chair,
So she can sit down while she combs her hair.
Hoppity-loppity, jump, one-two.
She has a pouch where her baby grows.
She carries the baby wherever she goes.
Hoppity-loppity, jump, one-two.
And when she jumps, she uses her tail,
So she can jump farther and almost sail.
Hoppity-loppity, jump, one-two.
*(Have children give two long jumps,
one short one on the word "jump",
and two quick jumps on the count "one-two.")*

Animals

This is the way the elephant goes
With curly trunk instead of a nose.
*(Clasp hands together, extend arms, and move
them back and forth.)*
The buffalo, all shaggy and fat,
Has two sharp horns in place of a hat.
(Place pointer fingers on forehead.)
The hippo with his mouth so wide
Let's you see what is inside.
*(Places hands together and open and close them to
simulate mouth movements.)*
The wiggly snake upon the ground
Crawls along without a sound.
(Weave hands back and forth.)
But monkey see and monkey do
Are the funniest animals in the zoo!
(Place thumbs in ears and wiggle hands.)

Counting at the Zoo

Count one, 1.
Come and have some fun!
Count two, 1, 2.
Let's run to the zoo!
Count three, 1, 2, 3.
A monkey's in a tree.
Count four, 1, 2, 3, 4.
Hear the animals roar.
Count five, 1, 2, 3, 4, 5.
Watch the porpoise dive.
Count six, 1, 2, 3, 4, 5, 6.
An ape is doing tricks.
Count seven, 1, 2, 3, 4, 5, 6, 7.
The giraffe is high as heaven.
*(As a finger play: point to a finger each time when
counting.)*
*(Suggest that the children add other animals to the
zoo or substitute lines such as: "Hear the lion
roar," "See the whooping crane stand in the rain,"
"See the big old moose. He must not get loose,"
"See the polar bear with white and furry hair.")*

Fun at the Zoo

One, one; the zoo is lots of fun!
*(Hold up hands with fingers extended;
bend down one finger.)*
Two, two; see a kangaroo!
(Bend down one finger.)
Three, three; see a chimpanzee!
(Bend down one finger.)
Four, four; hear the lions roar!
(Bend down one finger.)
Five, five; watch the seal dive!
(Bend down one finger.)
Six, six; there's a monkey doing tricks!
(Bend down one finger.)
Seven, seven; elephants eleven!
(Bend down one finger.)
Eight, eight; a tiger and his mate!
(Bend down one finger.)
Nine, nine; penguins in a line!
(Bend down one finger.)
Ten, ten; I want to come again!
(Bend down one finger; then clap hands.)

Monkey See, Monkey Do

A little monkey likes to do
Just the same as you and you;
When you sit up very tall,
Monkey sits up very tall;
When you pretend to throw a ball,
Monkey pretends to throw a ball;
When you try to touch your toes,
Monkey tries to touch his toes;
When you move your little nose,
Monkey moves his little nose;
When you jump up in the air,
Monkey jumps up in the air;
When you sit down in a chair,
Monkey sits down in a chair.
(Children follow actions of the rhyme.)

The Birthday Child

A birthday child had a birthday cake
With five candles burning bright.
   (Hold up five fingers.)
She blew out two of the candles,
How many still had light?
   (Hold up three fingers.)
How old is the birthday child? Do you know?
She is five years old. She told me so!
   (Hold up five fingers.)
   (Change the word "five" to "six" if appropriate.)

Four or Five Candles

Two candles,
   (Hold up two fingers on left hand.)
Two candles,
   (Hold up two fingers on right hand.)
That makes four.
I cannot see any more.
Four pretty candles, all the same—
Blow them out to play this game!
One *(blow)*, two *(blow)*, three *(blow)*, and four *(blow)*.
   (Blow on fingers as if blowing out candles.)
Are they all gone? Are there more?
Oh, yes, I see another one.
   (Hold up one finger.)
That makes five for birthday fun!
   (Hold up five fingers.)
Five pretty candles, all the same—
Blow them out to play this game!

My Birthday Cake

My birthday cake is _____ (*any color*) and white;
  (Make a circle with arms.)
The lighted candles make it bright;
1, 2, 3, 4, 5 pink candles!
  (Hold up fingers one by one to represent candles.)
What a pretty sight!
  *(Change the number of candles to correspond
  with child's age.)*

A Birthday

Today is _____'s birthday.
  (Insert the name of the child.)
Let's make her (him) a cake;
Mix and stir,
  (Action of stirring.)
Stir and mix,
Then into the oven to bake.
  (Pretend to hold cake in two hands.)
Here's our cake so nice and round;
  (Make a circle with arms.)
We frost it _____ (*any color*) and white;
  (Action of spreading frosting.)
We put _____ (*any number*) candles on it,
To make a birthday light.

Six Little Candles

Six little candles on a birthday cake;
  (Hold up six fingers.)
The flames look so alive.
You may blow one candle out!
Wh! And that leaves five!
  (Bend down one finger.)

Five little candles on a birthday cake;
  (Hold up five fingers.)
Just five, and not one more.
You may blow one candle out!
Wh! And that leaves four!
  (Bend down one finger.)

Four little candles on a birthday cake;
  (Hold up four fingers.)
As gay as they could be.
You may blow one candle out!
Wh! And that leaves three!
  (Bend down one finger.)

Three little candles on a birthday cake;
  (Hold up three fingers.)
Standing straight and true.
You may blow one candle out!
Wh! And that leaves two!
  (Bend down one finger.)

Two little candles on a birthday cake;
  (Hold up two fingers.)
Helping us have fun.
You may blow one candle out!
Wh! And that leaves one!
  (Bend down one finger.)

One little candle on a birthday cake;
It knows its task is done.
You may blow this candle out!
Wh! And that leave none!
  (Place hands behind back.)

("Wh" is a two-letter consonant speech sound which appears in such words as white, what, when, and where.)

Circus

Floppy Clown

I am a great big floppy clown.
(Flop.)
I bend away back; I bend away down.
(Bend body back and forth.)
I smile a big smile; and then I frown.
(Smile and frown.)
I am a great big floppy clown.
(Flop.)
I'm tired of flopping, so when I sleep
(Hands folded beside face.)
I'll fall down in a great big heap.
(Fall gently without making a sound.)

This Little Clown

This little clown is very fat;
(Hold up thumb.)
This little clown wears a silly hat;
(Hold up pointer finger.)
This little clown has a round, red nose;
(Hold up middle finger.)
This little clown has shoes with toes;
(Hold up ring finger and wiggle it.)
This little clown stands upside down.
(Hold up little finger.)
What is a circus without a clown!
(Clap hands.)

Ten Circus Wagons

Ten circus wagons, painted oh, so gay,
Came into town with the circus today!
(Hold up ten fingers.)
This one holds a lion
That gives a big, loud roar!
(Point to thumb on opposite hand.)
This one holds a tiger
Fast asleep upon the floor.
(Point to pointer finger.)
This one holds a funny seal
That nods to left and right.
(Point to middle finger.)
This one holds a zebra
That is striped all black and white.
(Point to ring finger.)
This one holds a camel
With two humps upon his back.
(Point to little finger.)
This one holds a panther
With his coat of fur so black.
(Point to thumb on other hand.)
This one holds an elephant
That is drinking from a pail.
(Point to pointer finger.)
This one holds a monkey
That is swinging by his tail.
(Point to middle finger.)
This one holds a hippo
With a grin so very wide.
(Point to ring finger.)
This one holds a leopard
With a gaily spotted hide.
(Point to little finger.)
Ten circus wagons, painted oh, so gay,
Came into town with the circus today!
(Hold up ten fingers.)

This Circus Clown

This circus clown shakes your hand.
(Shake hands.)
This circus clown plays in the band.
(Pretend to play flute.)
This circus clown has enormous feet.
(Show foot.)
This circus clown dearly loves to eat.
(Pretend to eat.)
This circus clown has a round red nose.
(Point to nose.)
This circus clown has white teeth in rows.
(Point to teeth.)
This circus clown has very sad eyes.
(Look sad.)
He laughs, and frowns, and then he cries.
(Demonstrate.)
This circus clown bends way down.
(Bend down.)
What would you do if you were a clown?

Floppety Clown

I am a clown and I don't care a bit
If my pants are pinned and my clothes don't fit.
(Pretend to hold up pants.)
Or if I have a great big toe.
(Show foot.)
(Children) 'Cause I'm a floppety clown, you know.

My arms are flippety, floppety, flap,
(Let arms flap.)
And my head bends down till it touches my lap.
(Bend.)
I twist my body. Look at it go!
(Twist right to left.)
(Children) 'Cause I'm a floppety clown, you know.

Somebody pulls me by a string.
(Stretch neck, pull upward with fingers.)
I open my mouth and start to sing.
(Open mouth.)
My legs are limp and they wobble so.
(Walk unsteadily.)
(Children) 'Cause I'm a floppety clown, you know.

Oh, I can frown and I can smile.
(Make expressions.)
I can stand on my head for a long, long while.
(Bend head down and touch floor with palms of hands.)
I flip and I flop from head to toe.
(Children) 'Cause I'm a floppety clown, you know.
(Bow.)

One Finger, Two

One finger, two fingers,
(Pop up small and ring fingers.)
Belong just to me.
Up pops a third one,
(Pop up middle finger.)
Now there are three.
Up pops a fourth one,
(Pop up pointer finger.)
Now there are four.
Up pops your thumb,
(Pop up thumb.)
Let's do it once more.

I See Three

I see three—one, two, three,
(Hold up three fingers one at a time.)
Three little bunnies
Reading the funnies.
I see three—one, two, three,
(Bend down three fingers one at a time.)
Three little kittens
All wearing mittens.
I see three—one, two, three,
(Hold up three fingers one at a time.)
Three little frogs
Sitting on logs.
I see three—one, two, three,
(Bend down three fingers one at a time.)
Three little bears
Climbing upstairs.
I see three—one, two, three,
(Hold up three fingers one at a time.)
Three little ducks
Riding on trucks.

Five Came Out to Play

Five little bugs came out to play.
1, 2, 3, 4, 5!
(Pop up fingers one at a time.)
They spied a bird and they ran away.
5, 4, 3, 2, 1!
(Bend down fingers one at a time.)
Five little birds came out for the air.
1, 2, 3, 4, 5!
They saw a cat and they flew out of there.
5, 4, 3, 2, 1!
Five little cats went out to the park.
1, 2, 3, 4, 5!
They saw a dog and were scared of his bark.
5, 4, 3, 2, 1!
Five little dogs heard a donkey cough.
1, 2, 3, 4, 5!
They turned on their tails and they scampered off.
5, 4, 3, 2, 1!
Six donkeys hid behind the trees,
(Hold hands behind back.)
When they heard the buzz of a swarm of bees.

Learning to Count

One, one; now we have begun;
(Hold up one finger.)
Two, two; shoes that are new;
(Hold up two fingers.)
Three, three; birds in a tree;
(Hold up three fingers.)
Four, four; blocks on the floor;
(Hold up four fingers.)
Five, five; bees in a hive;
(Hold up five fingers.)
Six, six; little drumsticks;
(Hold up six fingers.)
Seven, seven; clouds in the heaven;
(Hold up seven fingers.)
Eight, eight; cookies on a plate;
(Hold up eight fingers.)
Nine, nine; grapes on a vine;
(Hold up nine fingers.)
Ten, ten; let's all count again;
(Hold up ten fingers.)
1, 2, 3, 4, 5, 6, 7, 8, 9, 10.
(Bend fingers down one by one.)

Captain and Men

1, 2, 3, 4, 5 in a row.
(Pop up fingers one at a time on right hand.)
A Captain and his men!
And on the other side, you know,
Are 6, 7, 8, 9, and 10.
(Pop up fingers one at a time on left hand.)

One, Two, How Do You Do?

1, 2, how do you do?
1, 2, 3, clap with me;
1, 2, 3, 4, jump on the floor;
1, 2, 3, 4, 5, look bright and alive;
1, 2, 3, 4, 5, 6, your shoe to fix;
1, 2, 3, 4, 5, 6, 7, look up to heaven;
1, 2, 3, 4, 5, 6, 7, 8, draw a round plate;
1, 2, 3, 4, 5, 6, 7, 8, 9, get in line!
(Point to one finger at a time.)

Counting Action Rhyme

One, two; sit up. Please do!
(Children sit tall.)
Three, four; feet flat on the floor.
(Feet on floor.)
Five, six; stir and mix.
(Motion of stirring.)
Seven, eight; close the gate.
(Clap.)
Nine, ten; make a pen for a hen.
(Interlace fingers.)

Dive Little Goldfish

Dive, little goldfish one.
(Hold up one finger.)
Dive little goldfish two.
(Hold up two fingers.)
Dive, little goldfish three—
(Hold up three fingers.)
Here is food, you see!
(Sprinkling motion with fingers.)
Dive, little goldfish four.
(Hold up four fingers.)
Dive, little goldfish five.
(Hold up five fingers.)
Dive, little goldfish six—
(Hold up six fingers.)
I like your funny tricks.

Here Are Mother's Knives and Forks

Here are Mother's knives and forks;
(Interlock fingers, palms up.)
This is Father's table;
(Fingers interlocked, palms down.)
This is Sister's looking glass,
(Make peak of two pointer fingers.)
And this is Baby's cradle.
(Interlock fingers and rock back and forth; thumbs and little fingers should be extended.)
—*Traditional*

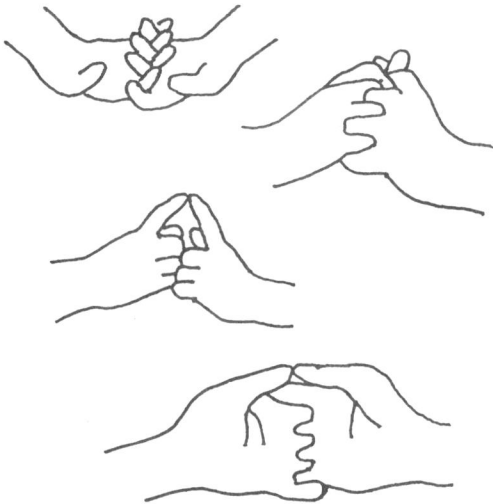

My Family

Here is my pretty mother;
(Point to pointer finger.)
Here is my father tall;
(Point to middle finger.)
Here is my older brother,
(Point to ring finger.)
And that isn't all;
Here is my baby brother,
(Point to little finger.)
As small as small can be.
Who is this other person?
(Point to thumb.)
Why, of course, it's ME!
1, 2, 3, 4, 5, you see,
(Touch each finger as you count.)
Make a very nice family!

These Are Grandmother's Glasses

These are Grandmother's glasses;
(Make a circle around each eye with fingers.)
This is Grandmother's cap;
(Hold fingers interlocked over head.)
This is the way she folds her hands,
(Fold hands.)
And lays them in her lap.
(Lay hands in lap.)
—*Traditional*

Here's a Cup of Tea

Here's a cup, and here's a cup,
(Make fist of left hand, then right hand.)
And here's a pot of tea;
(Add spout to right hand by protruding thumb.)
Pour a cup, and pour a cup,
(Pour into left and then right.)
And have a cup with me!
(Extend cup to neighbor and pretend to be drinking.)
—*Traditional*

The Farm

Counting at the Farm

One, one. A farm is lots of fun.
(Hold up thumb.)
Two, two. Hear the kitten mew.
(Hold up two fingers.)
Three, three. Birds are in a tree.
(Hold up three fingers.)
Four, four. Hear the puppy snore.
(Hold up four fingers.)
Five, five. Bees buzz in a hive.
(Hold up thumb and all fingers.)

Farmer Jones' Farm

One dog,
Two cats,
Three goats,
And four white rats.
Five hens,
Six cows,
Seven geese,
And eight sows.
Nine sheep,
Ten lambs,
And hidden away where nobody sees,
Are a hundred and fifty honey bees!
(The children hold up the required number of fingers each time.)

This Is the Farm

This is the meadow where every day
(Spread hands.)
Many farm animals come to play.
Here is the food that the farmer brings,
(Cup hands.)
Hay, oats, and corn, and other good things.
Here is a great, big watering trough.
(Measure with hands.)
They take a long drink and then scamper off.
(Fingers move.)
Here are the shears that shear the sheep,
(Movement of cutting.)
So that we might have blankets for sleep.
Here is the barn where they all unite
(Point fingers together.)
To rest themselves and sleep all night.

On the Farm

Here is a hungry piggie snout;
(Hold up thumb.)
He'd better stop eating, or his tail will pop out!
Here is busy Mother Hen;
(Hold up pointer finger.)
She likes to scratch for her chickens ten.
Here is a patient, friendly cow;
(Hold up middle finger.)
She's eating hay from a big haymow.
Here is Baa-Baa, a woolly sheep;
(Hold up ring finger.)
Her wool keeps me warm while I am asleep.
Here is funny, fuzzy cat;
(Hold up little finger.)
She likes to chase a mouse or rat.
(Move fingers to imitate a running cat.)

Five Little Chickens

Five little chickens by the old barn door;
(Hold up five fingers.)
One saw a beetle, and then there were four.
(Bend down one finger.)
Four little chickens under a tree;
One saw a cricket, and then there were three.
(Bend down one finger.)
Three little chickens looked for something new;
One saw a grasshopper; then there were two.
(Bend down one finger.)
Two little chickens said, "Oh, what fun!"
One saw a ladybug; then there was one.
(Bend down one finger.)
One little chicken began to run,
For he saw a katydid; then there were none!
(Bend down one finger.)

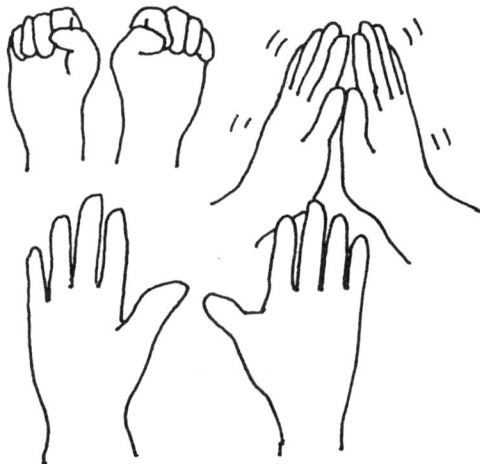

Ten Fluffy Chickens

Five eggs and five eggs,
(Hold up two hands.)
That makes ten;
Sitting on top is Mother Hen.
(Clap three times.)
What do I see?
Ten fluffy chickens
(Hold up ten fingers.)
As yellow as can be!

Cows on a Farm

This cow has a nose that is soft as silk.
This cow gives a pail of good sweet milk.
This cow switches flies with her long, thin tail.
This cow eats corn and hay by the bale.
This cow at night, sleeps inside a stall.
This cow has a baby calf very small.
The farmer says, "I don't know how
I could run this farm without a fine cow!"
(Point to one finger at a time.)

Five Little Goslings

One little gosling, yellow and new,
(Hold up one finger.)
Had a fuzzy brother, and that made two.
(Hold up two fingers.)
Two little goslings now you can see;
They had a little sister, and that made three.
(Hold up three fingers.)
Three little goslings waddled through the door;
Another sister got in line, and that made four.
(Hold up four fingers.)
Four little goslings went to swim and dive;
They met a little neighbor, and that made five.
(Hold up five fingers.)
Five little goslings; watch them grow!
(Spread hands wide apart.)
They'll turn into fine, big geese, you know!
(The word gosling may be changed to "duckling.")

Ten Little Ducklings

Ten little ducklings,
(Move hands back and forth in waddling motion.)
Dash, dash, dash!
Jumped in the duck pond,
(Motion of jumping.)
Splash, splash, splash!
When the mother called them,
"Quack, quack, quack,"
Ten little ducklings
(Hold up ten fingers.)
Swam right back.
(Motion of swimming.)

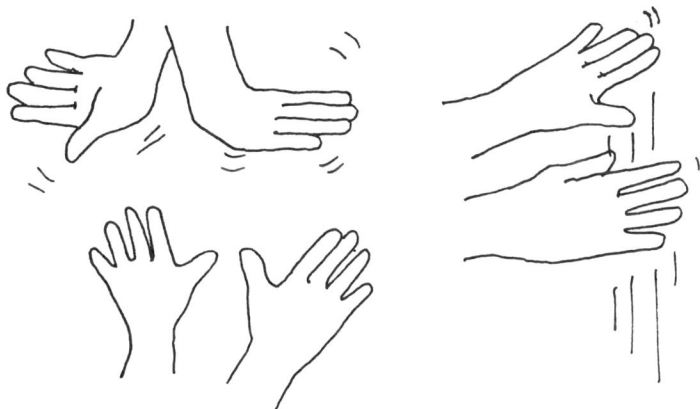

The Goose Family

Mr. Gander and Mrs. Goose,
(Hold up thumb and pointer finger on one hand.)
And their goslings, one, two, three,
(Hold up other three fingers on other hand.)
Are two and three, which make, you see,
A happy family.
Said Mr. Gander to Mrs. Goose,
(Bend down thumb and pointer finger.)
"The water's fine, I see;
We'll both go swimming, you and I,
With our babies, one, two, three."
(Bend down other three fingers.)

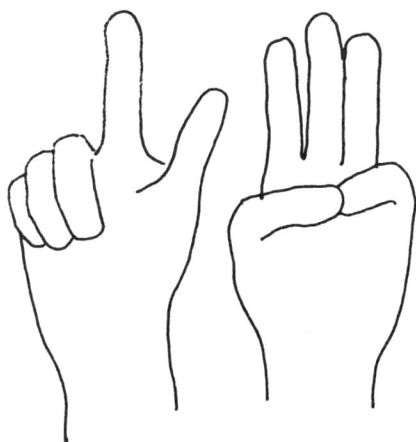

Five Little Pussy Cats

Five little pussy cats;
  (Hold up five fingers.)
See them play!
  (Wiggle fingers.)
This one is brown,
  (Bend down thumb.)
And this one is gray;
  (Bend down pointer finger.)
This one has a white nose;
  (Bend down middle finger.)
This one has sharp claws;
  (Bend down ring finger.)
This one has long whiskers
  (Bend down little finger.)
And tiny, soft paws.
1, 2, 3, 4, 5 pussy cats,
  (Pop up fingers as you count.)
Hurry away to scare the mice and rats.
  (Wiggle fingers.)
SQUEAK!
  (Clap hands.)
  —Adapted

Frisky Little Ponies

One little pony so full of fun
  (Hold up one finger.)
Likes to whinny and trot and run.
Two little ponies eat oats from a trough.
  (Hold up two fingers.)
And when they are full, they gallop off.
Three little ponies like their snacks
  (Hold up three fingers.)
Before they will give us rides on their backs.

Four Billy Goats

The first billy goat climbs on the roof.
The second billy goat taps with his hoof.
The third billy goat doesn't want to wait.
The fourth billy goat opens up the gate.
Four billy goats get into the garden
And don't even say, "I beg your pardon."
  (Point to one finger at a time.)

Six Young Roosters

Six young roosters began to play;
When all of a sudden, one ran away.
Five young roosters began to crow;
When all of a sudden, one hurt his toe.
Four young roosters went to the fair;
When all of a sudden, one wasn't there.
Three young roosters, and just as I feared;
All of a sudden, one disappeared!
Two young roosters pecked on the ground;
When all of a sudden, one couldn't be found.
One young rooster went to his nest;
When all of a sudden, he found all the rest.
  (Ask for volunteers to play the six roosters. They sit on a rug representing a set. One at a time leaves and at the end all return. All say the line "When all of a sudden," until they are more familiar with the rhyme.)

In My Little Garden

In my little garden with a lovely view,
Sunflowers are smiling, one and two.
In my little garden by the apple tree,
Daffodils are dancing, one, two, three.
In my little garden by the kitchen door,
Roses now are blooming, one, two, three, four.
In my little garden by the winding drive,
Violets are growing, one, two, three, four, five.
*(The children hold up required number
of fingers each time.)*

My Spring Garden

Here is my little garden.
(Make bowl shape with hands.)
Some seeds I am going to sow.
(Motion of scattering seeds.)
Here is my rake to rake the ground.
(Scratch with fingers.)
Here is my handy hoe.
*(Arms outstretched in front of body,
bend fingers downward.)*
Here is the big, round yellow sun,
(Make circle with arms.)
The sun warms everything.
Here are the rain clouds in the sky.
(Point to sky.)
The birds will start to sing.
(Move forefinger and thumb several times.)
Little plants will wake up soon,
(Stoop slowly and then raise.)
And lift their sleepy heads.
(Raise arms.)
Little plants will grow and grow
From their warm earth beds.

Five Little Seeds

Five little seeds, five little seeds,
(Hold up five fingers.)
Three will make flowers
(Hold up three fingers.)
And two will make weeds.
(Hold up two fingers.)
Under the leaves and under the snow,
Five little seeds are waiting to grow.
(Hold up five fingers.)
Out comes the sun,
(Make circle with arms.)
Down comes a shower.
(Raise arms and lower moving fingers.)
And up come the three pretty little pink flowers.
(Hold up three fingers.)
Out comes the sun
(Circle with arms.)
That every plant needs,
And up comes two funny, little, old weeds.
(Hold up two fingers.)

Flowers

Flowers tall,
(Let pointer and middle fingers stand up.)
Flowers small,
(Let little finger and thumb stand up.)
Count them one by one,
Blowing with the breezes
In the springtime sun!
1, 2, 3, 4, 5.
(Touch each finger as you count.)

I Am a Sunflower

I am a sunflower
Growing by the hour.
   (Children move slowly upward.)
Now I am grown,
And my petals full-blown.
   (Children stand tall.)
I turn to the right,
   (Turn head to right.)
And I face the light.
   (Make circle for sun.)
The sun sets in the West,
   (Turn head to left.)
And I have my rest.
   (Clasped hands beside face.)
I awake with the sun,
   (Make circle for sun.)
A new day has begun.

The Flower

Here's a green leaf,
   (Show hand.)
And here's a green leaf;
   (Show other hand.)
That, you see, makes two.
Here is a bud
   (Cup hands together.)
That makes a flower;
Watch it bloom for you!
   (Open cupped hands gradually.)

Things That Grow

Here is my little garden bed.
Here is one tomato ripe and red.
   (Hold up designated number of fingers.)
Here are two great, long string beans.
Here are three bunches of spinach greens.
Here are four cucumbers on a vine.
This little garden is all mine.

Relaxing Flowers

Five little flowers
Standing in the sun;
   (Hold up five fingers.)
See their heads nodding,
Bowing, one by one.
   (Bend fingers several times.)
Down, down, down
Comes the gentle rain,
   (Raise hands, wiggle fingers, and lower arms
   to simulate falling rain.)
And the five little flowers
Lift up their heads again!
   (Hold up five fingers.)

Small and Round

Small and round, small and round,
> (Make circle with thumb and pointer finger.)
A bulb is deep inside the ground.
> (Crouch to floor.)
Stretch and grow, stretch and grow;
> (Rise slowly.)
Up the stalk comes, slowly—slow.
Buds are seen, buds are seen.
> (Show fists.)
The petals grow 'mid leaves so green.
> (Release one finger at a time.)
Straight and tall, straight and tall,
> (Raise fingers high.)
Flowers grow beside the wall.
> (Lower fingers and cup palms
> for flowers.)

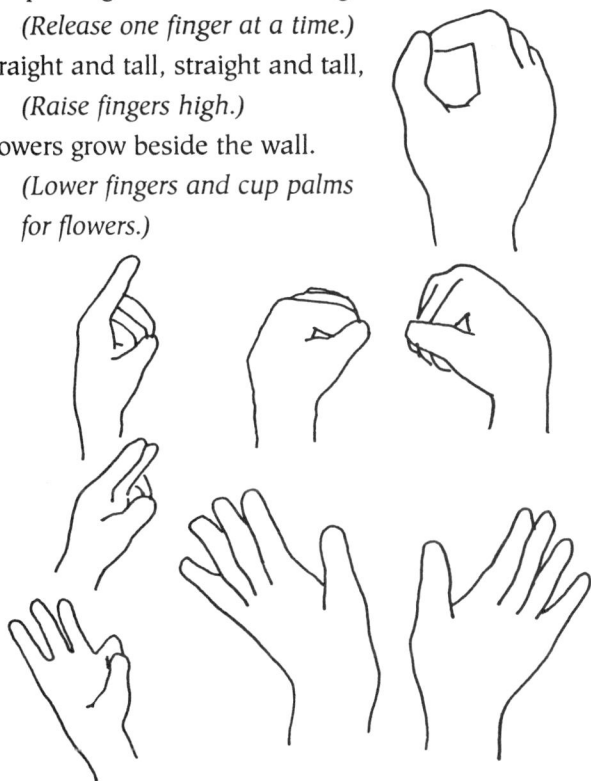

Pretending

I like to pretend that I am a rose
> (Cup hands.)
That grows and grows and grows and grows.
> (Open hands gradually.)
My hands are a rosebud closed up tight,
> (Close hands.)
With not a tiny speck of light.
Then slowly the petals open for me,
> (Let hands come apart gradually.)
And here is a full-blown rose, you see!

The Brown Seeds

Ten brown seeds lying in a straight row,
Said, "Now it is time for us to grow."
Up, up, up the first one shoots;
Up, up, up from its little seed roots.
Up, up, up the second one is seen;
Up, up, up in its little coat of green.
Up, up, up the third one's head
Comes up, up, up from its little earth bed.
Up, up, up the fourth one goes;
Up, up, up—we can see its little nose!
Up, up, up the fifth one pops;
Up through the soil and then it stops.
Up, up, up the sixth we see;
Up it comes and it looks at me.
Up, up, up the seventh one peeps!
Up, up, up through the soil it leaps.
Up, up, up the eighth we spy;
Up, up, up to stretch to the sky.
Up, up, up the ninth one springs;
Up, up, up and everything sings.
Up, up, up the tenth grows fast;
Up, up, up and it is the last.
Up, up, up—the seeds every one
Become ten plants to smile at the sun.
> (This rhyme demands fine body control. Have the children crouch down and one after the other rise slowly so that each seed's growth is not finished before that couplet ends. On the last two lines, all ten children stretch arms upward. Say, "Show how a seed looks when it is under the ground. You would curl up very small. Then slowly you would show one leg and arm at a time as you grow above the soil.")

Holidays

Ten Little Pumpkins

Ten little pumpkins all in a line;
   (Hold up ten fingers.)
One became a jack-o'-lantern,
Then there were nine.
   (Bend down one finger.)
Nine little pumpkins peeking through the gate;
An old witch took one,
Then there were eight.
   (Bend down one finger.)
Eight little pumpkins (there never were eleven);
A green goblin took one,
Then there were seven.
   (Bend down one finger.)
Seven little pumpkins full of jolly tricks;
A white ghost took one,
Then there were six.
   (Bend down one finger.)
Six little pumpkins glad to be alive;
A black cat took one,
Then there were five.
   (Bend down one finger.)
Five little pumpkins by the barn door;
A hoot owl took one,
Then there were four.
   (Bend down one finger.)
Four little pumpkins, as you can plainly see;
One became a pumpkin pie,
Then there were three.
   (Bend down one finger.)
Three little pumpkins feeling very blue;
One rolled far, far away,
Then there were two.
   (Bend down one finger.)
Two little pumpkins alone in the sun;
One said, "So long,"
And then there was one.
   (Bend down one finger.)

One little pumpkin left all alone;
A little boy chose him,
Then there were none.
   (Bend down last finger.)
Ten little pumpkins in a patch so green
Made everyone happy on Hallowe'en!

Four Big Jack-O'-Lanterns

Four big jack-o'-lanterns made a funny sight
Sitting on a gatepost Halloween night.
Number one said, "I see a witch's hat!"
Number two said, "I see a big, black cat!"
Number three said, "I see a scary ghost!"
Number four said, "By that other post!"
Four big jack-o'-lanterns weren't a bit afraid.
They marched right along in the Halloween parade.
   (Point to one finger at a time.)

Halloween Time

Halloween will soon be here.
It is now that time of year.
Can you be a big black cat?
Arch your back? Spit, spat, spat!
   (Make arch of arm.)
Can you be a pumpkin bright
And smile at me all through the night?
   (Make a circle with arms.)
Can you be a feathery owl
And look at me with a great big scowl?
   (Children frown.)
Can you be a scary ghost
Dancing all around a post?
   (Flop arms.)
BOO!

Three Turkey Gobblers

The day before Thanksgiving, as quiet as could be,
Three turkey gobblers sat up in a tree.
   (Hold up three fingers.)
The first turkey said, "I think that I will hide
Out behind the haystack for it is tall and wide."
   (Point to one finger at a time.)
The second turkey said, "I'll stay here in this tree,
And hide behind some branches where no one can see me."
The third turkey said, "I think I'll leave today,
For then the cook can't find me and put me on a tray."
And on Thanksgiving morning, when the farmer came to call,
The three turkey gobblers could not be found at all.

Pumpkin Head

My head is round,
   (Make a circle with arms.)
And so are my eyes.
   *(Make circles with thumbs and
   pointer fingers.)*
My nose is a triangle,
   (Draw a triangle in the air.)
Just this size.
My mouth is turned up
Like a shiny half-moon.
Upon your front porch
I'll be sitting quite soon.
Upon your front porch,
There I will be seen
Smiling at children
   (Children smile; point to smile.)
On this Halloween.

Turkey Walk

Old turkey gobbler walks very proudly;
Gobble, gobble, gobble,
   (Children repeat.)
Strut, strut, strut!
   (Children hold heads high and walk stiff-legged.)

When he walks, he gobbles very loudly;
Gobble, gobble, gobble,
Strut, strut, strut!

Hold your head high if you please;
Gobble, gobble, gobble,
Strut, strut, strut!

And when you walk, don't bend your knees;
Gobble, gobble, gobble,
Strut, strut, strut!

Five Yellow Pumpkins

The first yellow pumpkin said, "Oh, my!
I don't want to be a pumpkin pie."
　　(Hold up one finger at a time.)
The second yellow pumpkin said, "Oh, dear!
Something will happen to us, I fear."
The third yellow pumpkin said, "Oh, me!
I am as frightened as I can be."
The fourth yellow pumpkin said, "Let's go!
I won't be a jack-o'-lantern! No, no, no!"
The fifth yellow pumpkin said, "It's late!
I fear I will be served upon a plate."
The five yellow pumpkins rolled far away,
And could not be found Thanksgiving Day.
The man in the moon said, "Hooray for you!
It was time to go, and I'm glad you knew."

The Piñata

My goodness! My goodness!
A big paper jar!
　　(Make a large circle with hands.)
A big paper jar that is shaped like a star.
　　(Draw star shape in air.)
And filled full of walnuts and filled full of sweets,
　　(Cup hands.)
Of toys and of oranges and wonderful treats.
Let's hit it and hit it and hit it until
　　(Pretend to hit piñata.)
The piñata breaks and makes everything spill!
　　(Clap.)
OLÉ!
　　(Children cry "Olé" and pretend to pick up goodies.)

Christmas Secrets

I know so many secrets,
Such secrets full of fun;
But if you hear my secrets,
Please don't tell anyone.
　　(Whisper.)
Here are some lights that twinkle,
　　(Wiggle fingers.)
Here is an ornament.
　　(Make circle with fingers.)
Here is a great big present
　　(Measure length.)
From Grandpa it was sent.
And on the very tip-tip-top,
An angel you can see.
　　(Point up.)
What is the secret? Can't you tell?
Why, it's a Christmas tree!
　　(Stand and raise arms high.)

Happy New Year

On New Year's Day, on New Year's Day,
This is what I always say:
"Happy New Year, Daddy,
　　(Hold up pointer finger.)
Happy New Year, Mother,
　　(Hold up ring finger.)
Happy New Year, Sister,
　　(Hold up small finger.)
Happy New Year, Brother."
　　(Hold up thumb.)
On New Year's Day, on New Year's Day,
This is what I always say:
"HAPPY NEW YEAR!"

St. Patrick's Day

St. Patrick's Day is here, you see.
We'll pick some shamrocks, one, two, three.
　　(Hold up three fingers.)
We'll count the leaves and look them over,
And maybe find a four-leafed clover.
　　(Hold up four fingers.)
I'll sew green buttons on my vest.
　　(Point to chest.)
Green for St. Patrick is the best.
I'll wear a green hat, very high,
　　(Measure height.)
And dance a jig—at least I'll try.
　　(Shuffle feet.)

Making Valentines

In February, what shall I do?
I'll make some valentines for you.
The first will have a cupid's face;
The second will be trimmed with lace.
The third will have some roses pink;
The fourth will have a verse in ink.
The fifth will have a ribbon bow;
The sixth will glisten like the snow.
The seventh will have some lines I drew;
The eighth, some flowers—just a few.
The ninth will have three little birds;
The tenth will have three little words:
I LOVE YOU!
(Point to one finger at a time.)

Five Little Valentines

One little valentine said, "I love you."
(Hold up fist; extend one finger.)
Tommy made another; then there were two.
(Extend another finger.)
Two little valentines, one for me;
Mary made another; then there were three.
(Extend another finger.)
Three little valentines said, "We need one more."
Johnny made another; then there were four.
(Extend another finger.)
Four little valentines, one more to arrive;
Susan made another; then there were five.
(Extend another finger.)
Five little valentines all ready to say,
"Be my valentine on this happy day."

How Many Valentines?

Valentines, valentines;
How many do you see?
Valentines, valentines;
Count them with me:
One for Father,
(Hold up thumb.)
One for Mother,
(Hold up pointer finger.)
One for Grandma, too;
(Hold up middle finger.)
One for Sister,
(Hold up ring finger.)
One for Brother,
(Hold up little finger.)
And here is one for YOU!
(Make heart shape with thumbs and pointer fingers.)

I Had an Easter Bunny

I had an Easter bunny.
(Hold up one finger.)
One day she ran away.
I looked for her by moonlight.
(Hand shading eyes.)
I looked for her by day.
I found her in the meadow
With her babies 1, 2, 3.
(Point to one finger at a time.)
So now I have four rabbit pets
(Hold up four fingers.)
To run and jump with me.

Five Little Easter Eggs

Five little Easter eggs lovely colors wore;
(Hold up five fingers.)
Mother ate the blue one, then there were four.
(Bend down one finger.)
Four little Easter eggs, two and two, you see;
Daddy ate the red one, then there were three.
(Bend down one finger.)
Three little Easter eggs; before I knew,
Sister ate the yellow one, then there were two.
(Bend down one finger.)
Two little Easter eggs, oh, what fun!
Brother ate the purple one, then there was one.
(Bend down one finger.)
One little Easter egg, see me run!
I ate the very last one, and then there were none.
(Bend down last finger.)

Easter Rabbits

Five little Easter rabbits
(Hold up five fingers.)
Sitting by the door;
One hopped away, and then there were four.
(Bend down one finger.)

Refrain
Hop, hop, hop, hop;
(Clap on each hop.)
See how they run!
Hop, hop, hop, hop;
(Clap on each hop.)
They think it is great fun!

Four little Easter rabbits
(Hold up four fingers.)
Under a tree;
One hopped away, and then there were three.
(Bend down one finger.)
Repeat refrain.

Three little Easter rabbits
(Hold up three fingers.)
Looking at you;
One hopped away, and then there were two.
(Bend down one finger.)
Repeat refrain.

Two little Easter rabbits
(Hold up two fingers.)
Resting in the sun;
One hopped away, and there was one.
(Bend down one finger.)
Repeat refrain.

One little Easter rabbit
Left all alone;
He hopped away, and then there were none.
(Hand behind back.)

Refrain
Hop, hop, hop, hop!
(Clap on each hop.)
All gone away!
Hop, hop, hop, hop!
(Clap on each hop.)
They'll come back some day.
—*Unknown*

Houses

Two Little Houses

Two little houses closed up tight;
(Two closed fists.)
Open up the windows and let in the light.
(Spread hands apart.)
Ten little people tall and straight,
(Hold up ten fingers.)
Ready for the bus at half past eight!
(Fingers make running motion.)
—Unknown

Painting

Paint the ceiling, paint the door.
Paint the wall, and paint the floor.
Paint the roof—slush, slush, slush!
Paint the doorstep with your brush.
Now my house is done, you see.
You may come and visit me.
I've been working very hard
To paint my playhouse
In the yard.
(Sit on floor.)
(Pantomime the action of painting.)

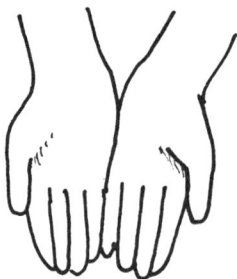

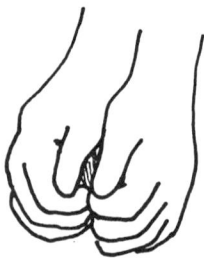

Windows

This house has many windows,
And some are very wide.
(Measure with hands.)
This one looks cross and frowning.
(Make frowning expression.)
You dare not look inside.
This window looks quite happy.
(More expressions.)
This window looks quite sad.
This window is so beautiful,
It makes us all feel glad.
This window has bright curtains.
This window looks so bare.
This window looks inviting.
I wonder who lives there!
(Point to one finger at a time.)

Houses

Here is a nest for the robin;
(Cup both hands.)
Here is a hive for the bee;
(Fists together.)
Here is a hole for the bunny;
(Finger and thumb make a circle.)
And here is a house for ME!
(Fingertips together to make a roof.)
—Unknown

Insects

Once I Saw a Beehive

Once I saw a beehive
  (Cup hands together to form hive.)
Out in the maple tree.
I said, "Little honeybees,
Come out and play with me!"
"Bzzzzzz!" went the honeybees
Inside the hive;
  (Motion of peeking inside hive.)
And then they came out—
One, two, three, four, five!
  (Show one finger at a time.)

This Little Cricket

The first little cricket played a violin.
The second little cricket joined right in.
The third little cricket made a crackly song.
The fourth little cricket helped him along.
The fifth little cricket cried, "Crick-crick-cree.
The orchestra is over and it's time for tea!"
  (Point to one finger at a time.)

Five Little Busy Bees

Five little busy bees on a day so sunny;
  (Hold up one hand, fingers extended.)
Number one said, "I'd like to make some honey."
  (Bend down first finger.)
Number two said, "Tell me, where shall it be?"
  (Bend down second finger.)
Number three said, "In the old honey-tree."
  (Bend down third finger.)
Number four said, "Let's gather pollen sweet."
  (Bend down fourth finger.)
Number five said, "Let's take it on our feet."
  (Bend down thumb.)
So the five little bees went buzzing along,
Humming their busy little honeybee song.
ZZZZZZZZZZZZZZZZZZZZZZZZZZZZ!

Little Ants

One little ant, two little ants,
Three little ants I see.
Four little ants, five little ants,
Lively as can be.
Six little ants, seven little ants,
Eight in a bowl of glass.
Nine little ants, ten little ants
Entertain our class.
  (Show the required number of fingers each time.)

The Little Caterpillars

Ten little caterpillars crawled up on a vine.
One slipped off and out of sight, and then there were _____.

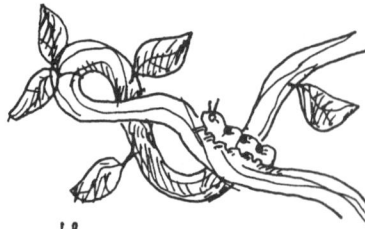

Nine little caterpillars sat upon the gate.
One hid behind the latch, and then there were _____.

Eight little caterpillars in a row quite even.
One went to find a leaf, and then there were _____.

Seven little caterpillars tried to find some sticks.
One went behind a bush, and then there were _____.

Six little caterpillars crawled down the drive.
One skittled far away, and then there were _____.

Five little caterpillars were creeping as before.
One slipped inside a crack and then there were _____.

Four little caterpillars climbed up a tree.
One hid behind some bark, and then there were _____.

Three little caterpillars found leaves that were new.
One crawled far out of sight and then there were _____.

Two little caterpillars were snoozing in the sun.
One woke up and dashed away, and then there was _____.

One little caterpillar, before the set of sun,
Turned into a butterfly and then there were _____.
*(The children hold up the required number of fingers
and supply the remaining number each time.)*

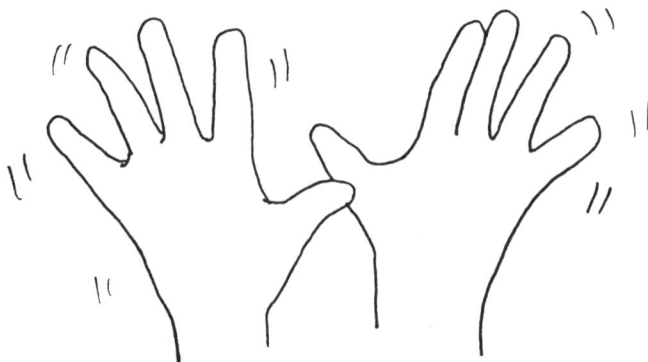

Sleepy Caterpillars

"Let's go to sleep," the little caterpillars said,
(Bend ten fingers into palms.)
As they tucked themselves into their beds.
They will awaken by and by,
(Slowly unfold and hold up fingers.)
And each one will be a lovely butterfly!
(Hands make flying motion.)

Counting Ladybugs

One, two, three, four, five,
   (Point to one finger at a time.)
Five little ladybugs walk down the drive.
Their coats are shiny and bright as stars.
They look like small, newly-painted cars.
One, two, three, four, five,
Five little ladybugs walk down the drive.

The Ladybugs

Tick-tack-tick-tack! See them go!
Four little ladybugs are marching in a row.
   (Hold up four fingers.)
The first one is yellow and trimmed with specks of black.
   (Point to one finger at a time.)
The second one is orange with a round and shiny back.
The third one is bright red with teeny, tiny dots.
The fourth one is fancy with different kinds of spots.
Ladybugs help ranchers. Ladybugs have use.
They eat up all the orange tree pests,
So we can have orange juice!

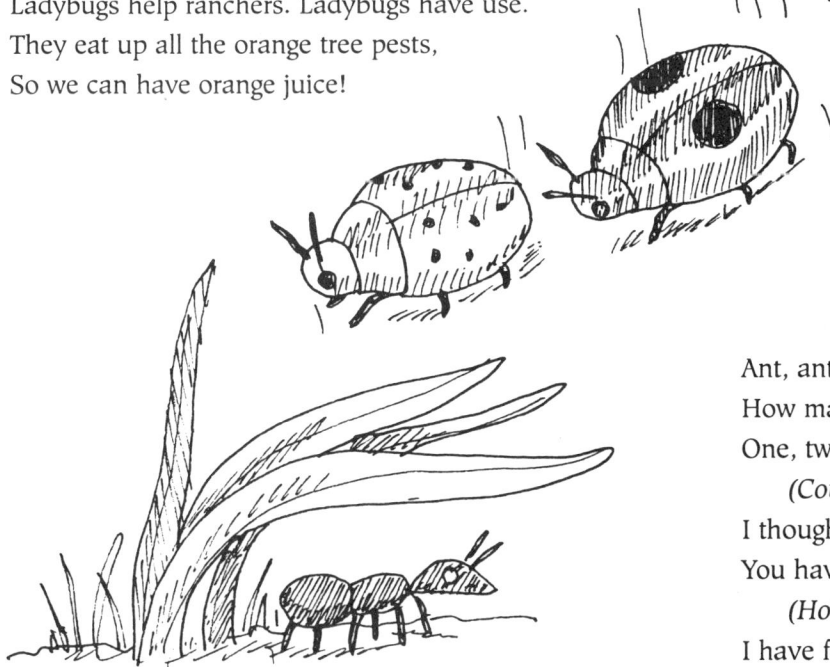

Ant under a Plant

Ant, ant, under a plant.
How many legs have you?
One, two, three, four, five, and six.
   (Count fingers.)
I thought you always knew.
You have two feet. You have two legs.
   (Hold up two fingers.)
I have four more legs than you.
   (Hold up four fingers.)

Ten Little Grasshoppers

Ten little grasshoppers swinging on a vine;
   (Hold up hands, fingers extended.)
One ate too many berries and then there were nine.
   (Bend down one finger.)

Nine little grasshoppers sitting on the gate;
One was blown away and then there were eight.
   (Bend down one finger.)

Eight little grasshoppers flying toward heaven;
One got lost upon a cloud and then there were seven.
   (Bend down one finger.)

Seven little grasshoppers lived between two bricks;
One said, "I'll hop away," and then there were six.
   (Bend down one finger.)

Six little grasshoppers glad to be alive;
One chased a bumblebee and then there were five.
   (Bend down one finger.)

Five little grasshoppers jumping on the floor;
One hid inside a crack and then there were four.
   (Bend down one finger.)

Four little grasshoppers saw a tiny flea;
One tried to chase it and then there were three.
   (Bend down one finger.)

Three little grasshoppers, and what did they do?
One skipped merrily away and then there were two.
   (Bend down one finger.)

Two little grasshoppers dancing in the sun;
One hid behind a tree and then there was one.
   (Bend down one finger.)

One little grasshopper, left all alone,
Hopped over the grass and then there were none.
   (Make fist.)
   *(The children may supply the remaining
   number each time.)*

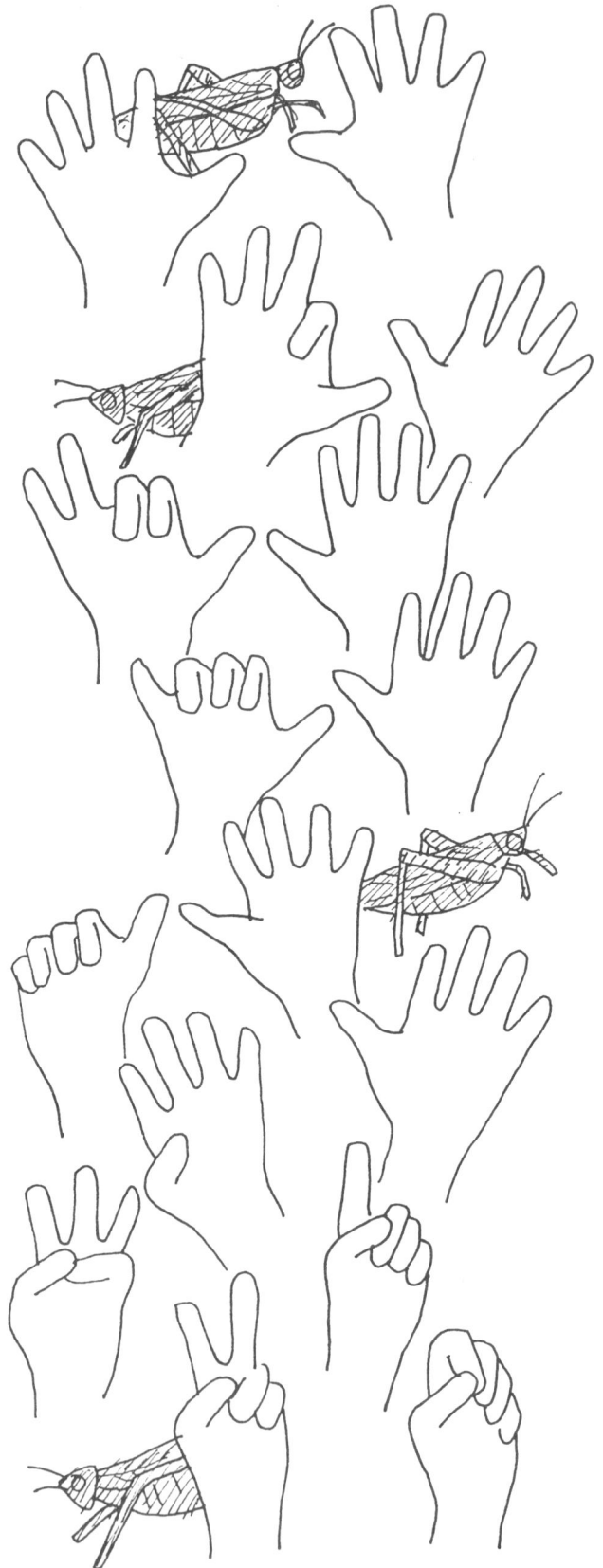

My Body

Touch Your Nose

Touch your nose,
Touch your chin;
That's the way this game begins.
Touch your eyes,
Touch your knees;
Now pretend you're going to sneeze.
    (Finger under nose.)
Touch your hair,
Touch one ear;
Touch your two red lips right here.
Touch your elbows
Where they bend;
That's the way this touch game ends.

Wiggles

A wiggle wiggle here,
A wiggle wiggle there,
Wiggle your hands up in the air.
Wiggle your shoulders,
Wiggle your hips,
Wiggle your knees,
And move your lips.
Wiggle, wiggle, wiggle,
And wiggle some more;
And now let's sit down on the floor.
    (Children follow actions of the rhyme.)

Stretch, Stretch

Stretch, stretch away up high.
    (Reach arms upward.)
Stretch and try to reach the sky.
    (Stand on tiptoes and reach.)
Be a bird, fly to a tree.
    (Motion of flying.)
Be a fish, swim in the sea.
    (Swim.)
Sway and sway just like a breeze.
    (Sway back and forth, with hip action.)
Now pretend you're going to sneeze!
    (Finger under nose.)

Ready to Listen

Let your hands go clap, clap, clap;
    (Clap hands three times.)
Let your fingers snap, snap, snap;
    (Snap fingers three times.)
Let your lips go very round,
    (Make lips round.)
But do not make a sound.
Fold your hands and close each eye;
    (Follow actions indicated.)
Take a breath . . . . and softly sigh:
Ah—!
    (Follow actions indicated.)

Fun with Hands

Roll, roll, roll your hands as slowly as can be;
Roll, roll, roll your hands;
Do it now with me.
Roll, roll, roll your hands as fast as fast can be;
Roll, roll, roll your hands;
Do it now with me.
    Continue this rhyme by substituting these phrases:
    Clap, clap, clap your hands.
    Shake, shake, shake your hands.
    Stamp, stamp, stamp your feet.

Finger Fun

One little finger wiggles in the sun.
Two little fingers run, run, run!
Three little fingers spread wide apart.
Four little fingers point to your heart.
Five little fingers walk up the hill.
Six little fingers stand straight and still.
Seven little fingers climb up a tree.
Eight little fingers fly like a bee.
Nine little fingers scratch in the sand.
All little fingers hide in my hand.
(Children follow actions of the rhyme.)

Me

Here are my fingers and here is my nose.
Here are my ears, and here are my toes.
Here are my eyes that are open and wide.
Here is my mouth with my white teeth inside.
Here is my pink tongue that helps me to speak.
Here are my shoulders and here is each cheek.
Here are my hands that will help me play.
Here are my feet that go walking each day.
(Point to each part of the body as it is mentioned.)

Hands on Shoulders

Hands on shoulders; hands on knees;
Hands behind you, if you please!
Touch your hips and touch your nose.
Bend way down and touch your toes.
Hands up high, now, in the air;
Down at sides, and touch your hair.
Hands up high as you did before.
Clap your hands: one, two, three, four!
(Children follow actions of the rhyme.)

Fingers and Toes

I have ten fingers,
(Hold up fingers.)
I have ten toes.
(Point to feet.)
They help very much as everyone knows!
I do not wish to have fins like a fish,
(Motion of swimming.)
Or paws like a dog,
(Double up fists.)
Or webs like a frog,
(Spread hands.)
Or claws like a bear,
(Curve fingers into claws.)
Or hooves like a mare,
(Double up fists, move fists up and down.)
Or scales like a snake,
Make no mistake!
I have ten fingers,
(Repeat motions.)
I have ten toes.
They help very much as everyone knows!
My fingers feel,
They can turn a wheel.
(Turn hand around.)
They can hold a cat,
(Cradle arms.)
Hit a ball with a bat.
(Hold imaginary bat with two hands.)
My toes like the sand,
And they help me to stand.
My toes can tiptoe,
And wade in the snow.
I have ten fingers,
(Hold up fingers.)
I have ten toes.
(Point to feet.)
They help very much as everyone knows!

Who Feels Happy Today?

Who feels happy at school today?
All who do, snap your fingers this way.
Who feels happy at school today?
All who do, clap your hands this way.
Who feels happy at school today?
All who do, wink your eyes this way.
Who feels happy at school today?
All who do, fold your hands this way.
> *(Children follow actions of the rhyme.)*

What I Can Do

I can spin just like a top.
Look at me! Look at me!
I have feet and I can hop.
Look at me! Look at me!
I have hands and I can clap.
Look at me! Look at me!
I can lay them in my lap.
Look at me! Look at me!
> *(The children act out this rhyme.)*

Active You

You wiggle your thumbs and clap your hands,
And then you stamp your feet.
You turn to the left, you turn to the right,
And make your fingers meet.
You raise them high and let them down;
You give another clap.
You wave your hands and fold your hands,
And put them in your lap.
> *(Follow directions for movements stated in the rhyme. Say the rhyme very slowly at first, since some children's coordination will not permit quick movements.)*

Thumbkins

Mr. Thumbkin Left and Mr. Thumbkin Right
> *(Hold up both thumbs.)*
Met each other on a Sunday night;
> *(Move thumbs together.)*
Mr. Thumbkin Left said, "How do you do?"
> *(Wiggle left thumb.)*
Mr. Thumbkin Right said, "Fine, and thank you!"
> *(Wiggle right thumb.)*
They began to yawn and to nod their heads,
> *(Move hands apart.)*
And they went back home to their cozy beds.
> *(Place hands behind back.)*

> *(Continue, substituting the words Mr. Pointer, Mr. Tall Man, Mr. Ring Man, and Mr. Wee Man.)*

Occupations

Four Busy Firefighters

Four busy firefighters could not retire
(Hold up four fingers.)
Because they might have to put out a fire.
The first one rang a big brass bell.
(Point to one finger at a time.)
The second one said, "It's the Grand Hotel!"
The third one said, "Down the pole we'll slide."
The fourth one said, "Get ready to ride."
The siren said, "Get out of the way!
We have to put out a fire today!"
The red fire truck speeded on to the fire,
As the big yellow flames grew higher and higher.
(Spread arms.)
Swish went the water from the fire hose spout,
And in no time at all, the fire was out.
(Rub palms together.)
The people all clapped and they gave a big yell:
"The firefighters saved our Grand Hotel!"
(Children may dramatize the rhyme.)

WHOOO - OOO

Five Little Firefighters

Five little firefighters sit very still
(Hold up five fingers.)
Until they see a fire on top of the hill;
Number one rings the bell, ding-dong;
(Bend down thumb.)
Number two pulls his big boots on;
(Bend down pointer finger.)
Number three jumps on the fire engine red;
(Bend down middle finger.)
Number four puts a fire hat on her head;
(Bend down ring finger.)
Number five drives the red fire truck to the fire,
(Bend down little finger.)
As the big yellow flames go higher and higher.
(Spread arms.)
Whooooo-ooooo! Whooooo-ooooo! hear the fire truck say,
(Imitate siren.)
As all of the cars get out of the way.
Shhhhh! goes the water from the fire hose spout,
(Rub palms together.)
And quicker than a wink the fire is out!
(Clap hands.)

The Dentist

When I try to count my teeth,
    (Point to teeth.)
I count and count and then,
I have to rest; I've done my best,
I counted up to ten.
One, two, three, four, five, six, seven,
    (Children point to teeth and count.)
Eight, nine, ten.
I then go to the dentist
And let her see my teeth.
    (Open mouth.)
She pumps the chair up to my size
With a pedal underneath.
Up and down the pedal goes,
    *(Raise hand up and down
    several times.)*
And so I take a ride.
And then I open up my mouth
    (Open mouth.)
So she can see inside.
She says to me, "Well, one, two, three,
    (Count on fingers.)
Four, five, six, seven, and eight.
It all looks fine except
Four teeth that must look straight."
    (Hold up four fingers.)
    *(Ask: What will happen to the four
    teeth that are not straight, but
    crooked? Have you ever known
    anyone to wear braces.)*

The Baker's Truck

The baker's truck comes down the street
Filled with everything good to eat;
Two doors the baker opens wide;
    (Stretch arms apart.)
Now, let us look at the shelves inside.
What do you see? What do you see?
    (Hands shading eyes.)
Doughnuts and cookies for you and me;
    (Make circles with thumbs and pointer fingers.)
Cinnamon rolls,
    (Make larger circles.)
And pies,
    (Make even larger circles.)
And bread, too;
What will he sell to me and to you?

I Want to be a Carpenter

I want to be a carpenter and work the whole day long.
I'll use a great big box of tools; my arms are very strong.
First, I'll saw and saw and saw, and cut the boards in two.
Little boards and big boards—all kinds of boards will do.
I'll plane and plane and plane the boards for every one is rough.
Back and forth I'll plane the boards until they're smooth enough.
I'll measure them and measure them—each one down to a T.
And then I'll start to build a house for me up in a tree!
    (Children pantomime the actions.)

Workers

This worker feeds the lions at the zoo.
This worker drives an engine to the fire.
This worker makes a new sole for your shoe.
This worker mends a high electric wire.
This worker drives a sweeper through the streets.
This worker bakes a cookie or a bun.
This worker sells my parents food to eat,
And I'm very glad we've got them, every one!

> *(Point to one finger at a time.)*
> *(Say, "Think of other people in the community
> who help us.")*

The Window Cleaner

Up goes the ladder to the side of the wall.
Don't worry! The window cleaner won't fall.
A window cleaner goes up to the top

> *(Fingers stimulate climbing by turning wrists
> and touching thumbs.)*

Up and on the last rung he'll/she'll stop.
He/she polishes the windows and makes them shine.
And when he/she is done, he/she will say,
"That is fine!"

Ten Clerks

One clerk works hard unpacking beans and rice.
Two clerks work hard arranging all the spice.
Three clerks work hard wrapping yellow cheese.
Four clerks work hard sorting drinks and teas.
Five clerks work hard marking all the jam.
Six clerks work hard slicing up the ham.
Seven clerks work hard packaging the sweets.
Eight clerks work hard selling all the meats.
Nine clerks work hard shelving rolls and bread.
Ten clerks worn out go home to bed.

> *(Show the correct number of fingers each time.)*

Telephone Line Workers

Over the towns and countryside
Telephone wires stretch far and wide.

> *(Hands measure width.)*

This first line worker climbs a pole

> *(Motion of climbing with hands.)*

With bravery and self-control.
The second wears goggles on his/her eyes

> *(Fingers encircle eyes.)*

In case some steel from wire flies.
The third one wears a belt with pride.

> *(Circle waist with two hands.)*

A safety belt is his/her best guide.
The fourth one climbs in cold and heat
With safe, strong climbers on both feet.

> *(Show feet one at a time.)*

The fifth, a telephone installs
Just so that you can make your calls.

> *(Hand to ear.)*
> *(This rhyme may be used as a finger play to review
> ordinal numbers.)*

Pets

Frisky's Doghouse

This is Frisky's doghouse;
(Pointer fingers touch to make a roof.)
This is Frisky's bed;
(Motion of smoothing.)
Here is Frisky's pan of milk
(Cup hands.)
So that he can be fed.
Frisky has a collar
(Circle neck with fingers.)
With his name upon it, too;
Take a stick and throw it,
(Motion of throwing.)
And he'll bring it back to you.
(Clap once.)

My Puppy

Here is a roof
(Point index fingers together.)
On top of a house.
(Place one hand on top of the other.)
Who lives here?
Is it a mouse?
Here is a collar.
(Hands encircle neck.)
Is it for a cat?
No, it's all for my puppy
So cuddly and fat.

Wiggling Puppies

One little puppy, one
Wiggled his tail and had wiggling fun.
(Wiggle finger.)
Two little puppies, two
Wiggled their bodies as puppies do.
(Wiggle whole self.)
Three little puppies, three
Wiggled their noses happily.
(Move nose.)
Four little puppies, four
Wiggled their shoulders and wiggled some more.
(Move shoulders.)
Five little puppies fat and round,
Wiggled their ears when they heard a sound.
(Choose five children who join the group, one at a time, as the rhyme is dramatized.)

Five Little Puppies

Five little puppies were playing in the sun;
(Hold up hand, fingers extended.)
This one saw a rabbit, and he began to run;
(Bend down first finger.)
This one saw a butterfly, and he began to race;
(Bend down second finger.)
This one saw a pussy cat, and he began to chase;
(Bend down third finger.)
This one tried to catch his tail, and he went round and round;
(Bend down fourth finger.)
This one was so quiet, he never made a sound.
(Bend down thumb.)

One Little Kitten, One

One little kitten, one
    (Hold up one finger.)
Said, "Let's have some fun!"
Two little kittens, two
    (Hold up two fingers.)
Said, "What shall we do?"
Three little kittens, three
    (Hold up three fingers.)
Said, "Let's climb up that tree."
Four little kittens, four
    (Hold up four fingers.)
Said, "Let's hide behind the door."
Five little kittens, five
    (Hold up five fingers.)
Said, "Here's a beehive!"
    (Make a fist with other hand.)
"Bzzzzzzzzz" went the bee,
And they scampered up a tree!
    (Move fingers in running motion.)

Little Kittens

Five little kittens playing on the floor;
    (Hold up five fingers.)
One smelled a mouse; then there were four.
Four little kittens, fat as fat could be;
    (Hold up four fingers.)
One saw a puppy; then there were three.
Three little kittens watched how birdies flew;
    (Hold up three fingers.)
One ran far up the tree; then there were two.
Two little kittens snoozing in the sun;
    (Hold up two fingers.)
One chased a rabbit; then there was one.
One little kitten looking for some fun;
    (Hold up one finger.)
He fluffed his tail and scampered off;
Now there isn't even ONE!

Sleepy Kitten

A kitten stretches.
    (Children stretch.)
And makes herself long.
    (Stretch again.)
Then she hums a soft
Little purring song.
    (Children whisper the word "purr" several times.)
She yawns a big yawn.
    (Children yawn.)
She stretches some more.
    (Children stretch again.)
And then she falls fast asleep on the floor.
    (Place palms together beside head.)

Six Little Fish

Six little fish, two in each pair,
    (Hold up two fingers.)
Coming up occasionally for a breath of air.
Two swim up, and two swim down;
    (Wiggle fingers.)
They swim in a circle around and around.
    (Draw a circle.)
Six come up.
They swim by threes.
But whenever I feed them, they don't say please.
Six little fish swim around, around.
They play tag with each other
And never make a sound.

Fred and His Fishes

Fred had a fishbowl.
In it was a fish,
    (Hold up one finger.)
Swimming around with a swish, swish, swish!
Fred said, "I know what I will do.
I'll buy another and that will make _____."
    (Children supply number and hold up two fingers.)
Fred said, "I am sure it would be
Very, very nice if I just had _____."
    *(Children supply number and hold up
    three fingers.)*
Fred said, "If I just had one more,
That would make one, two, three, _____."
    *(Children supply number and hold up
    four fingers.)*
Fred said, "What fun to see them dive,
One, two, three, four, _____."
    (Children supply number and hold up five fingers.)
How many fishes do you see?
How many fishes? Count them with me!
    (Children count to five.)
    (Repeat rhyme with a different child's name.)

Goldfish Pets

One little goldfish
Lives in a bowl.
Two little goldfish
Eat their food whole.
Three little goldfish
Swim all around.
Although they move,
They don't make a sound.
Four little goldfish
Have swishy tails.
Five little goldfish
Have pretty scales.
    (Show the correct number of fingers each time.)

My Pets

There are a lot of pets in my house.
I have one gerbil and one white mouse.
    (Hold up one finger on each hand.)
I have two kittens and two green frogs.
    (Hold up two fingers on each hand.)
I have three goldfish and three big dogs.
    (Hold up three fingers on each hand.)
Some folks say that is a lot!
Tell how many pets I've got.
    (Twelve.)
    *(You may make tally marks on the chalkboard
    for the numbers of pets and at the end of the
    rhyme children count them.)*

Five Little Seashells

Five little seashells lying on the shore;
  (Hold up five fingers.)
Swish! went the waves, and then there were four.
  (Show the action; bend down one finger.)
Four little seashells cozy as could be;
Swish! went the waves, and then there were three.
  (Show the action; hold up three fingers.)
Three little seashells all pearly new;
Swish! went the waves, and then there were two.
  (Show the action; hold up two fingers.)
Two little seashells sleeping in the sun;
Swish! went the waves, and then there was one.
  (Show the action; hold up one finger.)
One little seashell left all alone
Whispered "Shhhhhhhh" as I took it home.
  (Bend down last finger.)

Five Big Waves

I went to visit the beach one day,
And I saw five waves begin to play.
The first wave gave a great big swish!
The second wave washed up several fish.
The third wave washed away my boat,
And there I saw it was afloat.
The fourth wave washed away a shell.
The fifth wave made a little swell.
The five waves played with me all day,
And suddenly, they went away.
  *(This rhyme can be used as a finger play
  or acted out.)*

Going to the Seashore

I go to the seashore
In the warm sand.
I go wading with ten toes,
  (Hold up ten fingers.)
And oh, it feels grand.
I build a large castle
In the warm sand.
I shape it higher than my head
  (Measure height.)
With my own two hands.
  (Hold up hands.)

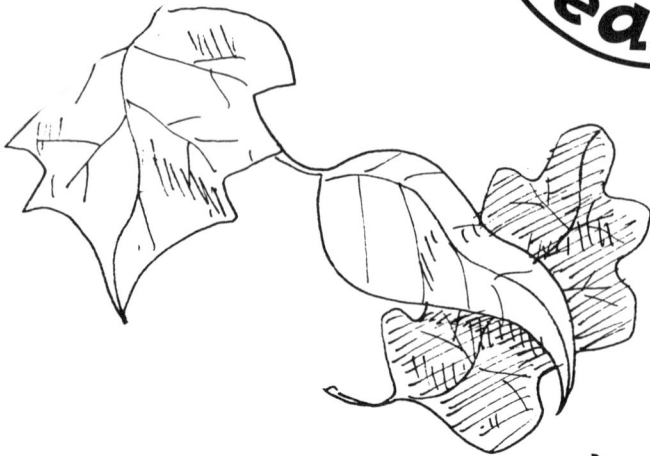

Raking Leaves

I rake the leaves
(Motion of raking.)
When they fall down
(Raise arms and let fingers fall gradually.)
In a great big pile.
(Measure width or height.)
And when there are enough of them,
I jump on them awhile.
(Give three jumps.)

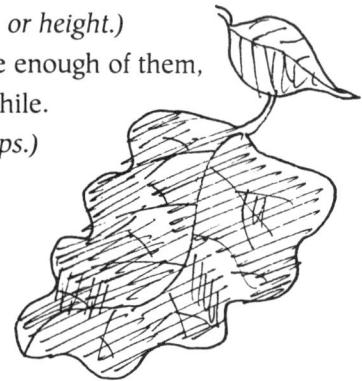

Little Leaves

Little leaves fall gently down,
Red and yellow, orange and brown;
(Raise hands and lower them, fluttering fingers like falling leaves.)
Whirling, whirling round and round,
(Repeat above motions.)
Quietly without a sound;
Falling softly to the ground,
(Lower bodies gradually to floor.)
Down—and down—and down—and down!

Fall Leaves

One leaf and two leaves
Tumbling to the ground,
Three leaves and four leaves
Make a rustling sound.
Five leaves and six leaves
Twirling all around,
Seven leaves and eight leaves
Whirling in a mound.
Nine leaves and ten leaves—
A north wind comes along,
And blows every leaf away
And that ends my song!
(The children hold up the required number of fingers each time.)

Three Little Oak Leaves

Three little oak leaves, red, brown, and gold,
Were happy when the wind turned cold.
(Hold up three fingers.)
The first one said, "I'll be a coat for an elf;
He'll be able to warm himself."
(Point to first finger.)
The second one said, "I'll be a home for a bug,
So he will be cozy and snug."
(Point to second finger.)
The third one said, "To a tiny seed I'll bring
A coat to keep it warm till spring."
(Point to third finger.)
Three little oak leaves, red, brown, and gold,
Were happy when the wind turned cold.
(Make motions for falling leaves.)

Scarecrow

Out in the meadow
A scarecrow stood.
  (Stand stiff with arms outstretched.)
His body was a stuffed coat.
His legs were made of wood.
His head had a straw hat
  (Hands on top of head.)
Very large and round.
  (Make circle with arms.)
His arms were two broom sticks
  (Hold up arms straight.)
And his feet were on the ground.
  (Stamp feet.)
His coat had ragged patches
  (Hands on thighs.)
They were faded and worn out.
He frightened all the crows
  (Flap arms up and down.)
That were flying all about.
You simply won't believe this,
But I will tell you that
Some birds had made a straw nest
Inside of his hat.
  (Cup hands for nest.)

Our Tenth Month

Wear a warm coat for autumn is here.
It is the tenth month of the year.
  (Hold up ten fingers.)
One for the cornfield,
  (Hold up one finger.)
Two for the leaves,
  (Hold up two fingers.)
Three for the cold rain that drips from the eaves.
  (Hold up three fingers.)
Four for the ponds that soon will freeze,
  (Hold up four fingers.)
And five for empty birds' nests in the trees.
  (Hold up five fingers.)
Wear a warm coat for autumn is here.
It is the tenth month of the year.
  (Hold up ten fingers.)

The Three Crows

One shiny crow sat up in a tree.
Caw, caw, caw!
Two shiny crows were as fat as could be.
Caw, caw, caw!
Three shiny crows ate from early morn.
Caw, caw, caw!
They ate every ear of the farmer's fresh corn.
Caw, caw, caw!
The scarecrow danced, and they all flew away.
Caw, caw, caw!
And said they would come back again the next day.
Caw, caw, caw!
  (Children hold up one finger at a time to represent the crows. The entire class says the refrain.)

Ten Little Snowpeople

One little, two little, three little snowpeople,
  (Extend three fingers, one at a time.)
Four little, five little, six little snowpeople,
  (Extend three more fingers, one at a time.)
Seven little, eight little, nine little snowpeople,
  (Extend three more fingers, one at a time.)
Ten little snowpeople bright.
  (Extend tenth finger.)

Ten little, nine little, eight little snowpeople,
  (Bend down three fingers, one at a time.)
Seven little, six little, five little snowpeople,
  (Bend down three fingers, one at a time.)
Four little, three little, two little snowpeople,
  (Bend down three fingers, one at a time.)
One little snowperson bright.
  (Bend down last finger.)

The Snowman

Roll a snowball large,
  (Arms make a circle.)
Then one of middle size;
  (Two pointer fingers and two thumbs make a circle.)
Roll a snowball small;
  (One pointer finger and thumb.)
Use lumps of coal for eyes.
  (Point to eyes.)
Place a carrot for a nose,
  (Point to nose.)
An old hat on his head,
  (Place both hands on top of head.)
And for his necktie, tie around
His neck a ribbon red.
  (Motion of tying ribbon.)
A corncob pipe goes in his mouth,
  (Point to mouth.)
Some buttons on his vest.
  (Point to buttons down front.)
And there he stands so round and fat;
Of snowmen, he's the best!

I Am a Snowman

I am a snowman, cold and white;
I stand so still all through the night,
  (Stand up tall.)
With a carrot nose,
  (Point to nose.)
And head held high,
And a lump of coal to make each eye.
  (Point to eyes.)
I have a muffler made of red,
And a stovepipe hat upon my head.
  (Place hands on top of head.)
The sun is coming out! Oh, my!
  (Make circle for sun.)
I think that I am going to cry;
  (Start sinking to floor.)
Yesterday, I was so plump and round;
Now I'm just a river on the ground.
  (Sink to floor.)

The Winter

The day is cloudy. The wind is bold.
(Hug body.)
Dress up warmly; you mustn't get cold.
Put on your coat, button up tight.
(Button coat.)
Put on your left boot, put on your right.
(Show each foot.)
Put on your scarf; put on your cap,
(Hands around neck and then top of head.)
Put on your mittens, and clap, clap, clap.
(Clap.)
Go out of doors and play and play.
Come in again, and then we will say:
Take off your coat buttoned up tight.
(Repeat the same motions as before.)
Take off your left boot, take off your right.
Take off your scarf, take off your cap,
Take off your mittens and have a short nap.
(Hands clasped beside face.)

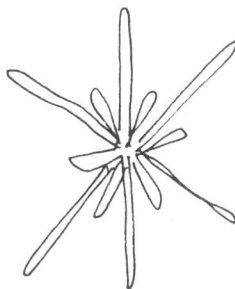

Mittens

Mittens for the snow time
When the world is white.
Mittens for my two hands,
(Hold up two hands.)
Mittens left and right.
(Indicate left and right.)
Mittens with a thumb place,
(Indicate thumb.)
Mittens warm and snug.
Mittens make me feel like
A bug inside a rug!
(Hug body.)

Groundhog Day

February second
(Hold up two fingers.)
Is Groundhog Day.
Will he see his shadow?
(Hands shading eyes.)
And what will he say?
If he says, "More cold,"
(Hug body.)
If he says, "More snow,"
(Raise arms and let fingers wiggle as they fall.)
Then into his hole
He will surely go.
(Fist behind back.)

Snowflakes in Our Town

The clouds are dark and in our town,
The flakes of snow are falling down.
One, two, three—they're falling fast.
(Hold up three fingers.)
Four, five, six—they'll never last.
(Hold up six fingers.)
Seven, eight, nine—they are so cold.
(Hold up nine fingers.)
Ten, eleven, twelve—all I can hold.
(Hold up ten fingers; stop and hold up two more.)
But, oh, here comes the happy sun!
They're melting!—twelve, eleven, ten, nine,
(Count backward.)
Eight, seven, six, five, four, three, two, one!

Spring Is Here!

Spring is here! Spring is here!
  (Clap four times.)
Winter is gone and two flowers appear.
  (Hold up two fingers.)
Three little robins begin to sing.
  (Hold up three fingers.)
Four bicycle bells begin to ring.
  (Hold up four fingers.)
Five children come out and jump the rope.
  (Hold up five fingers.)
Spring is here now! I hope, I hope!

Making Kites

The winds of March begin to blow,
And it is time for kites, you know.

Here's the way I make my kite;
Watch and help me do it right.

I cross two sticks, so thin and long,
  (Cross pointer fingers.)
Tied together good and strong;
  (Motion of tying.)

A string I fasten to each end,
  (Pretend to hold each side of kite.)
And across the middle to make it bend;

I measure and cut the paper gay,
  (Motion of measuring and cutting.)
And paste along the edge this way;
  (Motion of pasting.)

A ball of string to hold my kite,
  (Form circle with fingers.)
When it sails almost out of sight;

And here's my kite all ready to go!
  (Hands outstretched.)
Please, March Wind, begin to blow!

The Rain

Pitter-patter, raindrops,
Falling from the sky;
  (Wiggle fingers to imitate falling rain.)
Here is my umbrella
To keep me safe and dry!
  (Hands over head.)
When the rain is over,
And the sun begins to glow,
  (Make large circle with arms.)
Little flowers start to bud,
  (Cup two hands together.)
And grow and grow and grow!
  (Spread hands apart slowly.)

Five Little May Baskets

Five little May baskets waiting by the door;
(Hold up five fingers.)
One will go to Mrs. Smith, then there will be four.
(Bend down one finger.)

Four little May baskets, pretty as can be;
One will go to Mrs. Brown, then there will be three.
(Bend down one finger.)

Three little May baskets, one is pink and blue;
It will go to Mr. Jones, then there will be two.
(Bend down one finger.)

Two little May baskets, yellow as the sun;
One will go to Mr. Black, then there will be one.
(Bend down one finger.)

One little May basket; oh, it's sure to go
To my own dear mother, who's the nicest one I know.
(Cup hands to form basket.)

April Rain

Dance, little raindrops
(Children tap lightly on a book or a table.)
Tap with tiny feet.
The seeds will awaken
(Continue tapping.)
When they hear our beat.
Grow, little seeds
And see the cloudy sky.
(Children begin raising.)
Stretch, little roots
(Children stretch.)
You'll be a flower by and by.
(Cup hands above head.)
*(Children may enjoy making up a tune
for this rhyme.)*

Shapes

Draw a Circle

Draw a circle, draw a circle,
Round as can be;
    (Draw a circle in the air with pointer finger.)
Draw a circle, draw a circle
Just for me.

Draw a square, draw a square,
    (Draw a square in the air.)
Shaped like a door;
Draw a square, draw a square
With corners four.

Draw a triangle, draw a triangle
    (Draw a triangle in the air.)
With corners three;
Draw a triangle, draw a triangle
Just for me.

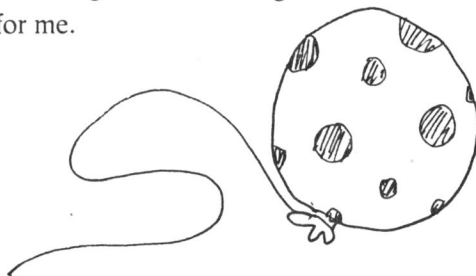

My Balloon

Here I have a new balloon.
    (Make circle with thumb and pointer finger.)
Help me while I blow;
Small at first, then bigger,
    (Make circle with thumbs and pointer fingers.)
Watch it grow and grow.
    (Make circle with arms.)
Do you think it is big enough?
Maybe I should stop;
For if I give another blow,
My balloon will surely POP!
    (Clap hands.)

Fingers, Fingers

Fingers, fingers everywhere,
Fingers drawing little squares,
Fingers drawing circles round,
Fingers drawing without a sound.
Fingers drawing rectangles,
Fingers drawing little bangles,
Fingers learning how to snap,
Fingers help hands clap, clap, clap!
    (Children draw shapes suggested in the air. Weave
    fingers for bangles, then give snaps and claps.)

Let's Make a Ball

A little ball,
    (Make a circle with pointer finger and thumb.)
A bigger ball,
    (Make a circle with both pointer fingers
    and thumbs.)
A great big ball I see;
    (Make large circle with arms.)
Now, let's count the balls we've made;
1, 2, 3.
    (Repeat actions of first three lines.)
    —Traditional

Trees

Leaf Buds in March

Ten little leaf buds grew upon a tree,
  (Hold up ten fingers.)
Curled up tightly as little buds should be.
  (Make two fists.)
Now the little leaf buds are keeping snug and warm,
All through the winter weather and the storm.
  (Wave hands back and forth.)
Along comes the cold and the windy month of March,
His breath is icy and it is strong and harsh.
He swings the little leaf buds very roughly, so,
  (Swing arms back and forth vigorously.)
Then very, very gently, he moves them to and fro.
  (Same arm movements, except slowly.)
Until the little raindrops fall down from the skies,
  (Raise arms and let moving fingers fall.)
And make the little leaf buds open up their eyes.
  *(Make two fists and let one finger at a time pop
  out to show ten buds.)*

The Nut Tree

Five brown chestnuts fell from the tree.
  (Hold up five fingers.)
I thought that the chestnuts were only for me.
But one was taken home by a girl.
  (Hold up four fingers.)
And one was taken home by a squirrel.
  (Hold up three fingers.)
A chipmunk took one to her nest.
  (Hold up two fingers.)
I hurried up and took all the rest.
  (Hold up one finger.)
I planted one nearby, you see.
Someday, we'll have a new nut tree!
  (Raise arm high.)

The Apple Tree

Away up high in an apple tree,
  (Point up.)
Two red apples smiled at me.
  (Form circles with fingers.)
I shook that tree as hard as I could;
  (Pretend to shake tree.)
Down came those apples,
And mmmmm, were they good!
  (Rub tummy.)
  —Traditional

The Airplane

The airplane has great big wings;
(Arms outstretched.)
Its propeller spins around and sings,
(Make one arm go around.)
"Vvvvvv!"
The airplane goes up;
(Lift arms.)
The airplane goes down;
(Lower arms.)
The airplane flies high
(Arms outstretched, turn body around.)
Over our town!

Here is the Engine

Here is the engine on the track;
(Hold up thumb.)
Here is the coal car, just in back;
(Hold up pointer finger.)
Here is the boxcar to carry freight;
(Hold up middle finger.)
Here is the mail car. Don't be late!
(Hold up ring finger.)
Way back here at the end of the train
(Hold up little finger.)
Rides the caboose through the sun and the rain.

Ten Little Tugboats

Ten little tugboats are out on the sea
And that is where little tugboats should be.

Ten little tugboats got along fine,
Till one drifted far away, and then there were _____.

Nine little tugboats said, "We can't wait."
One went too far out, and then there were _____.

Eight little tugboats were lined up quite even.
One couldn't keep the pace, and then there were _____.

Seven little tugboats, before you could say "ticks,"
One got lost in the fog and then there were _____.

Six little tugboats had a lot of drive.
But one tooted out to sea, and then there were _____.

Five little tugboats said, "Let's move to shore."
But one backed up from the rest, and then there were _____.

Four little tugboats were sailing evenly.
One hit a big barge, and then there were _____.

Three little tugboats said, "We'll carry through."
But one lost its engine, and then there were _____.

Two little tugboats said, "We'll make the run."
But one lost its smokestack, and then there was _____.

One little tugboat pulled a ship to shore.
That tugboat was successful, and now there are no more.

Wheels

Wheels, wheels, wheels go around, around
(Twirl hands.)
Bicycles need wheels to move along the ground.
Are wheels ever square? No, they are round.
(Circle with hands.)
Wheels, wheels, wheels go around, around.
(Twirl hands again.)

Raindrops

Raindrops, raindrops!
Falling all around;
  (Move fingers to imitate falling rain.)
Pitter-patter on the rooftops,
  (Tap softly on table or floor.)
Pitter-patter on the ground.
Here is my umbrella;
It will keep me dry;
  (Hands over head.)
When I go walking in the rain,
I hold it up so high.
  (Raise hands in air.)

Puddles

One puddle, two puddles
Made by the rain.
Three puddles, four puddles
Down in the lane.
Five puddles, six puddles
We can wade through.
Seven puddles, eight puddles
Quite muddy, too!
Nine puddles, ten puddles
Covering tiny roots.
Eleven puddles, twelve puddles—
We all need our boots.
  *(Have twelve children represent puddles. Each one
  stands when number is called.)*

The Rain Cloud

There's a rain cloud in the sky.
  (Point to sky.)
Now it's drifting down.
  (Raise arms, move fingers and lower them.)
Slowly, slowly raindrops fall
  (Repeat motion.)
Covering the town.
Splish, splosh, splatter, plop!
Raindrops splatter as they drop.
Go inside and don't get wet.
There are lots of splashes yet.
Get your slicker or your coat,
  (Put on imaginary coat.)
Run and find your little boat.
Put on your boots, put on your cap,
  (Continue motions.)
Zip yourself up with a snap!
Splash in puddles, slosh in rain.
  (Move hands up and down.)
Watch the rain run down the drain.
Now, come play and sail your boat.
  (Wave hand to one side.)
The rain has stopped, take off your coat.
  (Remove imaginary garments.)
Take off your boots, take off your cap,
Zip off your jacket with a snap.
Now lie down for a cozy nap.
  (Stretch out on floor.)

I Am the Wind

I toss the kites up in the sky,
   (Sweep hand upward.)
And help the people's clothes to dry.
I send down leaves in golden showers,
   (Raise arm, move fingers, and lower them.)
And make warm blankets for the flowers.
   (One hand over other.)
And then again, the seeds I sow
Change little raindrops into snow.
   (Raise hands, move fingers.)
I pile the snow in drifts at night,
   (Raise hands high.)
Till all the world looks cold and white.
And when the setting sun is red,
   (Make circle of arms.)
I quiet down and go to bed.
   (Palms together beside face.)

Little White Clouds

One little white cloud
   (Hold up one finger.)
Played tag in the breeze.
Two little white clouds
   (Hold up two fingers.)
Looked down at the trees.
Three little white clouds said,
   (Hold up three fingers.)
"Hi!" to a plane.
Four little white clouds smiled
   (Hold up four fingers.)
And greeted a train.
Five little white clouds
   (Hold up five fingers.)
Turned to dark grey,
And began to cry on the earth today.
   (Raise fingers in air and lower them gently.)

Umbrellas

I put on my raincoat.
   (Pretend to put on coat.)
I put on my hat.
   (Put on hat.)
I put up my umbrella
   (Fingertips touching over head.)
Just like that!
Umbrellas go up,
Umbrellas go down,
   (Point up and down.)
When rain clouds are dark
All over the town.
One raindrop and two,
   (Hold up one finger at a time.)
Two raindrops and three,
My up and down umbrella
Is up over me.
   (Fingertips touching over head.)
Four raindrops and five,
   (Hold up one finger at a time.)
Six raindrops and seven,
Raindrops are tumbling
   (Raise arms and let fingers fall slowly.)
Down from the heaven.
Drip, drip, drip, drip!
I am dry as can be,
My up and down umbrella
Is up over me.
   (Fingertips touching over head.)